Modern Language Association of Americ

Approaches to Teaching
World Literature

Joseph Gibaldi, Series Editor

1. Joseph Gibaldi, ed. *Approaches to Teaching Chaucer's* Canterbury Tale
2. Carole Slade, ed. *Approaches to Teaching Dante's* Divine Comedy. 1982.
3. Richard Bjornson, ed. *Approaches to Teaching Cervantes'* Don Quixote. 1984.
4. Jess B. Bessinger, Jr., and Robert F. Yeager, eds. *Approaches to Teaching* Beowulf. 1984.
5. Richard J. Dunn, ed. *Approaches to Teaching Dickens'* David Copperfield. 1984.
6. Steven G. Kellman, ed. *Approaches to Teaching Camus's* The Plague. 1985.
7. Yvonne Shafer, ed. *Approaches to Teaching Ibsen's* A Doll House. 1985.
8. Martin Bickman, ed. *Approaches to Teaching Melville's* Moby-Dick. 1985.
9. Miriam Youngerman Miller and Jane Chance, eds. *Approaches to Teaching* Sir Gawain and the Green Knight. 1986.
10. Galbraith M. Crump, ed. *Approaches to Teaching Milton's* Paradise Lost. 1986.
11. Spencer Hall, with Jonathan Ramsey, eds. *Approaches to Teaching Wordsworth's Poetry*. 1986.
12. Robert H. Ray, ed. *Approaches to Teaching Shakespeare's* King Lear. 1986.
13. Kostas Myrsiades, ed. *Approaches to Teaching Homer's* Iliad *and* Odyssey. 1987.
14. Douglas J. McMillan, ed. *Approaches to Teaching Goethe's* Faust. 1987.
15. Renée Waldinger, ed. *Approaches to Teaching Voltaire's* Candide. 1987.
16. Bernard Koloski, ed. *Approaches to Teaching Chopin's* The Awakening. 1988.
17. Kenneth M. Roemer, ed. *Approaches to Teaching Momaday's* The Way to Rainy Mountain. 1988.
18. Edward J. Rielly, ed. *Approaches to Teaching Swift's* Gulliver's Travels. 1988.
19. Jewel Spears Brooker, ed. *Approaches to Teaching Eliot's Poetry and Plays*. 1988.
20. Melvyn New, ed. *Approaches to Teaching Sterne's* Tristram Shandy. 1989.
21. Robert F. Gleckner and Mark L. Greenberg, eds. *Approaches to Teaching Blake's* Songs of Innocence and of Experience. 1989.
22. Susan J. Rosowski, ed. *Approaches to Teaching Cather's* My Ántonia. 1989.
23. Carey Kaplan and Ellen Cronan Rose, eds. *Approaches to Teaching Lessing's* The Golden Notebook. 1989.
24. Susan Resneck Parr and Pancho Savery, eds. *Approaches to Teaching Ellison's* Invisible Man. 1989.
25. Barry N. Olshen and Yael S. Feldman, eds. *Approaches to Teaching the Hebrew Bible as Literature in Translation*. 1989.
26. Robin Riley Fast and Christine Mack Gordon, eds. *Approaches to Teaching Dickinson's Poetry*. 1989.
27. Spencer Hall, ed. *Approaches to Teaching Shelley's Poetry*. 1990.

28. Sidney Gottlieb, ed. *Approaches to Teaching the Metaphysical Poets.* 1990.
29. Richard K. Emmerson, ed. *Approaches to Teaching Medieval English Drama.* 1990.
30. Kathleen Blake, ed. *Approaches to Teaching Eliot's* Middlemarch. 1990.
31. María Elena de Valdés and Mario J. Valdés, eds. *Approaches to Teaching García Márquez's* One Hundred Years of Solitude. 1990.
32. Donald D. Kummings, ed. *Approaches to Teaching Whitman's* Leaves of Grass. 1990.
33. Stephen C. Behrendt, ed. *Approaches to Teaching Shelley's* Frankenstein. 1990.
34. June Schlueter and Enoch Brater, eds. *Approaches to Teaching Beckett's* Waiting for Godot. 1991.
35. Walter H. Evert and Jack W. Rhodes, eds. *Approaches to Teaching Keats's Poetry.* 1991.
36. Frederick W. Shilstone, ed. *Approaches to Teaching Byron's Poetry.* 1991.
37. Bernth Lindfors, ed. *Approaches to Teaching Achebe's* Things Fall Apart. 1991.
38. Richard E. Matlak, ed. *Approaches to Teaching Coleridge's Poetry and Prose.* 1991.
39. Shirley Geok-lin Lim, ed. *Approaches to Teaching Kingston's* The Woman Warrior. 1991.
40. Maureen Fries and Jeanie Watson, eds. *Approaches to Teaching the Arthurian Tradition.* 1992.
41. Maurice Hunt, ed. *Approaches to Teaching Shakespeare's* The Tempest *and Other Late Romances.* 1992.
42. Diane Long Hoeveler and Beth Lau, eds. *Approaches to Teaching Brontë's* Jane Eyre. 1993.
43. Jeffrey B. Berlin, ed. *Approaches to Teaching Mann's* Death in Venice *and Other Short Fiction.* 1992.
44. Kathleen McCormick and Erwin R. Steinberg, eds. *Approaches to Teaching Joyce's* Ulysses. 1993.
45. Marcia McClintock Folsom, ed. *Approaches to Teaching Austen's* Pride and Prejudice. 1993.
46. Wallace Jackson and R. Paul Yoder, eds. *Approaches to Teaching Pope's Poetry.* 1993.
47. Edward Kamens, ed. *Approaches to Teaching Murasaki Shikibu's* The Tale of Genji. 1993.
48. Patrick Henry, ed. *Approaches to Teaching Montaigne's* Essays. 1994.
49. David R. Anderson and Gwin J. Kolb, eds. *Approaches to Teaching the Works of Samuel Johnson.* 1993.

Approaches to Teaching the Works of Samuel Johnson

Edited by

David R. Anderson

and

Gwin J. Kolb

The Modern Language Association of America
New York   1993

Library of Congress Cataloging-in-Publication Data

Approaches to teaching the works of Samuel Johnson / edited by David
    R. Anderson and Gwin J. Kolb.
        p.   cm.   —   (Approaches to teaching world literature ; 49)
    Includes bibliographical references and index.
    ISBN 0-87352-721-6 (cloth) ISBN 0-87352-722-4 (pbk.)
    1. Johnson, Samuel, 1709–1784 — Study and teaching. 2. Johnson,
    Samuel, 1709–1784 — Criticism and interpretation. I. Series.
    PR3537.S78A66   1993
    828'.609 — dc20   93-11790

Cover art for the paperback edition: illustration from *The R. B. Adam Library
Relating to Samuel Johnson and His Era*, vol. 1, London, 1929.

Published by The Modern Language Association of America
10 Astor Place, New York, New York 10003-6981

Printed on recycled paper

CONTENTS

PREFACE TO THE SERIES

In *The Art of Teaching* Gilbert Highet wrote, "Bad teaching wastes a great deal of effort, and spoils many lives which might have been full of energy and happiness." All too many teachers have failed in their work, Highet argued, simply "because they have not thought about it." We hope that the Approaches to Teaching World Literature series, sponsored by the Modern Language Association's Publications Committee, will not only improve the craft — as well as the art — of teaching but also encourage serious and continuing discussion of the aims and methods of teaching literature.

The principal objective of the series is to collect within each volume different points of view on teaching a specific literary work, a literary tradition, or a writer widely taught at the undergraduate level. The preparation of each volume begins with a wide-ranging survey of instructors, thus enabling us to include in the volume the philosophies and approaches, thoughts and methods of scores of experienced teachers. The result is a sourcebook of material, information, and ideas on teaching the subject of the volume to undergraduates.

The series is intended to serve nonspecialists as well as specialists, inexperienced as well as experienced teachers, graduate students who wish to learn effective ways of teaching as well as senior professors who wish to compare their own approaches with the approaches of colleagues in other schools. Of course, no volume in the series can ever substitute for erudition, intelligence, creativity, and sensitivity in teaching. We hope merely that each book will point readers in useful directions; at most each will offer only a first step in the long journey to successful teaching.

Joseph Gibaldi
Series Editor

PREFACE TO THE VOLUME

There are some obvious reasons for making the writings of Samuel Johnson a central part of the English curriculum: he wrote one of the first dictionaries of the English language; he was one of the early editors of the greatest poet in English, Shakespeare; he prepared an edition of the English poets that represents one of the original attempts to erect and justify a canon in English literature. Someone who played so central a role in fixing meaning to words and assigning value to verbal constructs belongs, it can be argued, in every student's curriculum.

The genesis and rationale of this volume, however, derive from another source: our perception, born of our own experiences and those of colleagues who kindly responded to a questionnaire on Johnson, that students enjoy studying him. His writings speak directly to the concerns of undergraduates, who find in Johnson not only material for study but also challenging and thought-provoking ideas for living. Johnson writes perceptively and feelingly about the quest for identity and vocation; about our relation to authority in the church, the state, and the family; about the relations between the sexes; about the operations of the mind and of the imagination and their effect on our daily lives; and about our choice of what to read and how to read it. Above all, however, he focuses on the problem of knowing how to live and living according to that ideal.

These topics capture the attention and imagination of undergraduates, and in this volume we show how successful teachers and scholars across the country have made those topics come alive in their classrooms. Their conceptual models and practical tips are intended both for experienced teachers of Johnson and for those who teach him rarely or not at all. As the essays attest, Johnson can be taught in a broad range of courses and in a wide variety of formats, and we have deliberately structured our book to emphasize this fact.

After our brief survey of the materials available to teachers of Johnson, the first section of this book offers general or thematic approaches to his writings. These discussions by Catherine N. Parke on Johnson and gender, James G. Basker on Johnson and authority, Timothy Erwin on Johnson and Locke, William Kupersmith on Johnson as a stylist, and Gloria Sybil Gross on psychoanalytic approaches to Johnson are not tied to specific works; rather, they discuss the relation of Johnson's life and writings to broad themes and concepts. The essays describe how Johnson can be successfully taught in contexts other than the standard literary history course, such as a writing course, a women's studies course, and a course on psychoanalysis and literature.

We also present two stimulating essays on teaching Johnson in the survey course. Raymond-Jean Frontain's essay on teaching Johnson in the British survey course begins with the novel approach of reserving Johnson until the second half of the survey, using his writings as a starting point for the study of Romantic and modern literature. Ann Engar offers a model for teaching Johnson in the broadest kind of survey, a history of Western civilization that emphasizes the play of ideas across history.

In the largest section of this book, we include nine essays on teaching specific works of Johnson. The essays by Charles H. Hinnant on the *Life of Savage*, Lawrence Lipking on the *Lives of the Poets*, Melvyn New on *Rasselas*, and Stephen Fix on Johnson's critical writings treat the Johnsonian texts taught most often and will, we hope, inspire new approaches and a reinvigorated presentation of them. The other essays in this section — Brenda Ameter's on the political writings, Bruce Redford's on the letters, Allen Reddick's on the *Dictionary*, Thomas F. Bonnell's on the Soame Jenyns review, and Thomas Jemielity's on *A Journey to the Western Islands* — discuss works that, though less well known, occupy important places in Johnson's canon and, more to the point, function well in the classroom. As these essays demonstrate, the riches of Johnson's writings are not exhausted by the frequently anthologized pieces. Students respond with warmth and interest to the lesser-known Johnson as well as to the familiar one; these essays should encourage teachers across the country to experiment with Johnson's canon in constructing their own syllabi.

According to our survey, the writings of Samuel Johnson are widely taught at colleges and universities throughout the country, and the essays in this volume testify to the variety of uses to which Johnson's works are put. We hope that this volume will further energize an already vigorous community of teachers and learners to achieve rich and rewarding classroom interactions with the writings of Samuel Johnson.

DRA and GJK

ACKNOWLEDGMENTS

We wish to acknowledge with gratitude those who have assisted us in the preparation of this volume. Joseph Gibaldi, editor of the MLA's Approaches to Teaching World Literature series, has encouraged and wisely counseled us from the beginning of this project. We deeply appreciate his support and the good advice of the anonymous readers for the MLA who reviewed our manuscript. The Department of English at Texas A&M University, under the leadership first of Hamlin Hill and then of J. Lawrence Mitchell, backed our project with the resources that enabled distant editors to work together. We are particularly grateful for assistance with word processing from Tracy Elias, Renae Fitzpatrick, and Barbara Butler. Our colleagues listed at the end of this volume responded generously to our questions about their teaching of Samuel Johnson's works, providing copies of syllabi, assignments, and examinations and practical advice of many kinds. We hope that the result will reward their efforts.

Part One

MATERIALS

Classroom Texts: The Teacher, the Anthology, and the Canon

David R. Anderson

Johnsonians around the country have generously responded to our inquiries about which texts they teach at various levels and which classroom anthologies they use. This essay reports their answers and explores the implications of those answers for the study of Johnson by undergraduates at American and Canadian colleges and universities. In brief, we have learned that Johnson is widely taught at a variety of levels to undergraduates, that a few anthologies dominate the classroom (the particular anthology a student is likely to encounter depends on the level of the course), and that the choice of anthology determines which Johnsonian texts students will encounter. Thus the compilers and publishers of anthologies play a key role in determining which works students are likely to read.

We have found that Johnson is typically taught in three kinds of classes: the introductory survey of English literature, the mid-level survey of eighteenth-century British literature, and the upper-level seminar on Johnson or the age of Johnson. For the lower-level survey course the anthology of choice is volume 1 of *The Norton Anthology of English Literature* (ed. Abrams et al.), often because its use provides consistency with other departmental offerings at that level but also because it is both consistently available and reasonably priced. For the mid-level survey course in eighteenth-century British literature, the most popular text is Geoffrey Tillotson, Paul Fussell, Jr., and Marshall Waingrow's *Eighteenth-Century English Literature* (hereafter cited as Tillotson), because of the breadth of its selections and the quality of its background material. In upper-level courses that focus on Johnson or that use individual texts for individual authors, three Johnson anthologies predominate: Bertrand Bronson's *Samuel Johnson:* Rasselas, *Poems, and Selected Prose* (now out of print but mentioned prominently by our respondents); Frank Brady and W. K. Wimsatt's *Samuel Johnson: Selected Poetry and Prose*; and Donald Greene's *Samuel Johnson* in the Oxford Authors series.

According to our respondents, the two Johnsonian texts taught most often in the introductory survey course are *Rasselas* and *The Vanity of Human Wishes*. The fifth edition of *The Norton Anthology* (1986) included, for the first time in the Norton compilations, all of *Rasselas*, and many of our respondents indicate that this change enabled them to teach that work in their introductory survey courses for the first time. It is gratifying to see that *Rasselas*, which is particularly relevant to undergraduate readers, is being more widely taught; however, it is significant that many students will now know *Rasselas* chiefly because it has become available in the standard anthology for introductory survey courses. When asked which Johnsonian works they taught in the introductory course, our respondents often answered, "All the works in the *Norton.*" This pattern suggests that other works will remain untaught at the introductory level largely because they do not appear in the *Norton,* which contains *The Vanity of Human Wishes* but not *London*; selections from the Lives of Cowley, Milton, and Pope but not from the *Life of Savage*; *Rambler* no. 4 on fiction but none of the *Ramblers* on pastoral.

The *Norton* seems to stress Johnson's poetry and criticism more than it does his moral writing. It presents some of Johnson's best poetry in a variety of modes: *Vanity,* the "Prologue Spoken by Mr. Garrick," "On the Death of Dr. Robert Levet," and the "Short Song of Congratulation." Similarly, the *Norton* provides a brief but representative sampling of Johnson's criticism through excerpts from the Preface to Shakespeare, selected *Lives of the Poets,* and *Rambler* nos. 4 and 60. These selections work best in a course that emphasizes the pattern of English literary history rather than the achievement of individual writers. However, readers will come away from the *Norton* with a more sparing sense of Johnson the moralist. They will know *Vanity* and *Rasselas* but not the great *Ramblers* in which Johnson's moral vision receives perhaps its most profound and sympathetic expression. There is no other widely used introductory anthology cited by respondents to our questionnaire. Instructors wishing to teach more or other Johnsonian texts at this level typically order a separate Johnson anthology or assign reading from library reserve lists.

Johnson naturally figures prominently in mid-level eighteenth-century survey courses around the country. In these classes, the Tillotson anthology dominates, principally — according to our respondents — because of its scope. The Johnsonian texts most often taught include *The Vanity of Human Wishes* and other poems, *Rasselas,* selected *Ramblers* and *Idlers,* selected *Lives of the Poets,* the *Life of Savage,* and — less often — selections from the *Dictionary,* from Johnson's private writings, from *A Journey to the Western Islands of Scotland,* and the review of Soame Jenyns's *Free Inquiry.* The anthology used in this course is again crucial in determining what students are asked to know about Johnson. In some respects, the *Norton* and the Tillotson are very similar. Except for two short works, Tillotson et al. print the same Johnson poems that appear in the *Norton Anthology.* Like the *Norton,* they give *Rasselas* in its entirety. Although they provide a slightly different selection from the *Lives of the Poets,* one of which — the Life of Gray — is complete, their view of the *Lives* is substantially the same.

However, the Tillotson anthology offers both more depth and more breadth than the *Norton* does. It contains, for example, a considerably longer extract from the Preface to Shakespeare. And, unlike the *Norton,* which includes four periodical essays, it has fourteen *Rambler* essays and two *Idlers.* Some areas unrepresented in the *Norton* — extracts from the Soame Jenyns review, from Johnson's prayers and meditations, and from his letters — are covered by Tillotson. (One anomaly: it ignores the *Dictionary*, which is represented in the *Norton*.)

Thus the instructor who adopts, as most of our respondents do, the Tillotson text in the mid-level eighteenth-century survey course can present a Johnson different from the one represented in the leading text for an introductory course. In our view, the Tillotson anthology offers more space to Johnson the moralist, particularly through its inclusion of more periodical essays; it also presents Johnson's personal writing in greater abundance. By devoting fully one-quarter of its Johnson pages to the prayers and meditations and to the letters, Tillotson's anthology calls students' attention to the connections between Johnson's writing and his life.

There is also an important difference between Tillotson and the *Norton* in the handling of Boswell. Though both the *Norton* and Tillotson print selections from Boswell immediately after the selections from Johnson, their choices vary significantly. The *Norton*'s extract from the *Life of Johnson* is rather lengthy; Tillotson excludes Boswell's Johnson from its pages, emphasizing instead Johnson's inner life as depicted in his own words. In place of extracts from the *Life*, Tillotson includes extracts from Boswell's journal (also represented in the *Norton*) and from the *Journal of a Tour to the Hebrides*.

We encountered in our respondents' comments on the Tillotson anthology the same phenomenon displayed in their comments on the *Norton*: instructors tend to let the anthology determine what they will teach. When asked in reference to a given course, "Please indicate which works you teach," respondents often answer, "All the works excerpted in Tillotson." Those who do supplement the anthology with other texts typically look for fuller representation of the *Lives of the Poets*, and our respondents frequently complained of the lack of a consistently available, moderately priced edition of the *Lives*.

Important differences also exist among the three leading Johnson anthologies used in upper-level courses on Johnson and his circle. (As noted earlier, one of these texts, Bronson's anthology of Johnson, is now out of print, but it received such prominent mention in the responses to our survey and represents such a clearly focused view of Johnson that we are including it in this discussion.) Greene gives the broadest view of Johnson the writer, because he includes the most texts. His anthology is particularly strong in Johnson's political writing, an area not represented in either of the others. Bronson, by his attention to the personal writing and his selections from the periodical essays, gives a more limited but perhaps also more focused view of Johnson, emphasizing Johnson the moralist. Brady and Wimsatt offer an even more specific reading of Johnson. Through the space they give to the *Lives of the Poets* and their selections from the periodical essays, they stress Johnson the critic. In choosing one of these anthologies over the other, therefore, an instructor is perforce leaning toward a particular portrait of Johnson the man and the writer.

The best sense of how these anthologies differ emerges from a comparison of how they choose to represent Johnson. All three anthologies print *Rasselas*, the Preface to Shakespeare, and the preface to the *Dictionary*. In all three, space is given to Johnson's personal writing, but Greene and Bronson both present generous samples while Brady and Wimsatt publish only some letters. Although all three works contain Johnson poems, Greene offers an abundant selection from Johnson's poetry (including an extract from *Irene*), while Bronson, and Brady and Wimsatt, limit themselves to roughly the same number of poems as the *Norton*. The three compilations devote equal space to the periodical essays. However, Bronson prints mainly moral *Ramblers* (e.g., nos. 5, 25, 32, 50, 134, 204, 205, none of which appears in Brady and Wimsatt) while the Brady and Wimsatt volume presents mainly critical numbers (e.g., 36, 37, 94, 156, 158, none of which appears in Bronson). On the whole, Greene selects different *Ramblers* from the other two anthologies, but the choices are not as obviously focused on one or the other kind of writing. Brady and Wimsatt have included six of the *Lives of the Poets* in their entirety (Cowley, Milton, Swift, Pope, Collins, Gray) and the *Life of Savage*, a selection that occupies nearly half their anthology. In Bronson there are the Lives of Pope, Savage, and Gray in their entirety and seven extracts. For his part, Greene has only two complete Lives (Addison and Collins) and eight extracts. The list of Johnsonian texts that appear only in Greene is too long to print here, but it includes such significant texts as "A Complete Vindication of the Licensers of the Stage," "The Vision of Theodore," specimen entries from the *Dictionary*, "Observations on the Present State of Affairs" and "The Patriot," and selections from the Vinerian Lectures on the English law. Our respondents are almost evenly divided over which anthology they prefer. Those who prefer the Greene anthology praise its broad inclusiveness. Those who prefer the Bronson anthology point to its focus on what they see as the key works. Adherents of the Brady and Wimsatt work note its generous and complete selection from the *Lives of the Poets*. One distinguished Johnsonian suggested that for an upper-level age of Johnson course, either the Bronson compilation or the Brady and Wimsatt anthology is most suitable because these courses allow only a limited time for Johnson; in a Johnson seminar, however, the Greene is most appropriate because of its breadth. It seems to us that text selection at this level depends very much on the instructor's own view of Johnson and on his or her own scholarly and critical interests. In the introductory or mid-level courses, where one anthology dominates, instructors tended to report dissatisfaction with the available selections. At the upper level, with two fine anthologies available, we observed more general satisfaction among those who used these texts and fewer instances in which the anthology was dictating what the instructor taught.

Instructors who wish to teach Johnson to undergraduates at any level will find a reasonable selection of anthologies in which his work is well represented. However, these anthologies, like all texts, must be approached critically, with an eye to both what they contain and what they omit. There are Johnsonian texts, like *Rasselas* until the fifth edition of *The Norton Anthology*, that are not being taught, especially to beginning undergraduates, simply because they do not appear in the classroom anthology. In the essays that follow, our contributors show a number of ways to avoid the tyranny of an anthology, and we invite our readers to consider them.

Scholarly and Critical Resources

Gwin J. Kolb

This essay is largely based on responses to the survey of teachers of Johnson's works and on my personal estimate of a number of publications that have proved to be exceedingly valuable in my more than forty years of teaching courses on Johnson (both undergraduate and graduate). Some titles noted below are also mentioned in one or more of the essays in the Approaches section of this volume.

Hoping to increase the essay's usefulness to likely readers, I have arranged the initial — and longest — two parts in an order paralleling, roughly, the seven succeeding sections; that is, I describe general studies first and then essays and books on more restricted topics, particularly examinations of kinds of works and of specific works. Later parts list miscellaneous publications, biographies, background studies, scholarly editions, literary histories, bibliographies, and nonprinted materials.

General Studies and Collections of Discrete Essays

Among older discussions, two — Walter Raleigh's *Six Essays on Johnson* (1910) and David Nichol Smith's "Johnson and Boswell" (1913) — present exceptional cases for the remarkable worth and vitality of Johnson's compositions. The latter had been peremptorily dismissed by Thomas Babington Macaulay in his notorious, and very influential, review of John Wilson Croker's edition of Boswell's *Life of Johnson* (1831) and subsequently rated far below Johnson the man in Macaulay's biography (frequently reprinted, like his review of Croker) in the eighth edition of the *Encyclopaedia Britannica* (1856).

Of post–World War II studies, the first to be cited — Walter Jackson Bate's *Achievement of Samuel Johnson* — demonstrates beyond a doubt Johnson's greatness as a member of our species and argues convincingly, often eloquently, for the extraordinary grasp of human nature and experience exhibited in his prose and poetry. Donald Greene's *Samuel Johnson* provides an incisive account of Johnson's life and his exceedingly diverse accomplishments as a man of letters. Paul Fussell's *Samuel Johnson and the Life of Writing* likewise treats astutely the often neglected truth that, virtually from the beginning to the end of his career, Johnson was a versatile professional author laboring in the London publishing marketplace. Isobel Grundy's *Samuel Johnson and the Scale of Greatness* treats perspicaciously the recurring, multifaceted concept of human greatness, usually involving mensuration and comparison, in Johnson's works. And Alvin Kernan's wide-ranging *Printing Technology, Letters, and Samuel Johnson* also focuses primarily, as its title suggests, on Johnson as a writer, formed by, and operating within, a print culture.

Like the general studies described above, the collections of discrete essays listed here all appeared after World War II. *The Age of Johnson*, a festschrift for Chauncey Brewster Tinker edited by Frederick W. Hilles, includes only three articles on Johnson, but the other thirty-three discuss many major figures and literary attainments of the period. *New Light on Dr. Johnson*, also edited by Hilles, consists of twenty essays — mostly scholarly — dealing with various aspects of Johnson's life and compositions. *Samuel Johnson: A Collection of Critical Essays*, edited by Greene, reprints fifteen pieces (among them F. R. Leavis's "Johnson as Critic") that examine almost as many different topics. *Johnson, Boswell, and Their Circle*, a festschrift for L. F. Powell edited by Mary Lascelles et al., contains twenty previously unpublished essays — seventeen on Johnson and three on Boswell. *Eighteenth-Century Studies in Honor of Donald F. Hyde*, edited by W. H. Bond, devotes ten essays to Johnsonian subjects, thirteen to non-Johnsonian. *The Unknown Samuel Johnson*, edited by John J. Burke, Jr., and Donald Kay, prints nine papers — unified by a common goal of increasing our knowledge of the unfamiliar Johnson — that were given in earlier versions during a 1983 symposium at the University of Alabama. *Johnson after Two Hundred Years*, edited by Paul J. Korshin, assembles, under three headings ("Johnson's Life," "Johnson's Intellectual Development," and "Interpretations of Johnson's Works"), fourteen papers of which all but one were delivered during a 1984 conference at Pembroke College, Oxford, commemorating the two-hundredth anniversary of Johnson's death. Similarly, *Fresh Reflections on Samuel Johnson*, edited by Prem Nath, brings together twenty-three essays, covering both the life and works, that were intended to memorialize the bicentennial of Johnson's death.

Works on Specific Topics

Prose Style

When teachers decide to include selections from Johnson's works in their courses, most of them apparently favor his poetry, moral writings (preeminently the periodical essays and *Rasselas*), philological tracts, letters, literary criticism, and biographies — but not necessarily in this order. Whatever their choices of texts, most instructors also apparently devote at least a brief amount of time to Johnson's prose style, perhaps the most distinctive, surely among the most celebrated, in English letters. Thus two books by William K. Wimsatt, Jr. — *The Prose Style of Samuel Johnson* and *Philosophic Words: A Study of Style and Meaning in the* Rambler *and* Dictionary *of Samuel Johnson*, which supply expert guidance in the dissection of the elements of Johnson's prose — appropriately precede the following groups of works.

Poetry

No full-length discussion of Johnson's entire poetic corpus has yet appeared. Limited estimable studies include T. S. Eliot's introduction to an edition of *London* and *The Vanity of Human Wishes*, David Nichol Smith's "Samuel Johnson's Poems," F. R. Leavis's "Johnson as Poet," Howard D. Weinbrot's assessment of *London* and *The Vanity of Human Wishes* in *The Formal Strain: Studies in Augustan Imitation and Satire*, John Wain's "Dr. Johnson's Poetry," and Thomas Jemielity's "Samuel Johnson, *The Vanity of Human Wishes*, and Biographical Criticism." Also, a number of the essays in the collections edited by Hilles (*New Light*), Greene (*Collection*), Bond, and Nath (listed under "General Studies" above) and part of Leopold Damrosch's *Samuel Johnson and the Tragic Sense* (cited below under "Literary Criticism") examine the poetry, notably *London* and *The Vanity of Human Wishes*.

Moral Writings

As even casual readers of Johnson might have guessed, numerous books and articles have examined the writings, along with related compositions and subjects, that have most obviously earned for Johnson the epithet the Great Moralist. In this category, the books rated highest — to judge from frequency of mention — by the respondents to our questionnaire are Robert Voitle's *Samuel Johnson the Moralist*; Maurice J. Quinlan's *Samuel Johnson: A Layman's Religion*; Paul Kent Alkon's *Samuel Johnson and Moral Discipline*; Arieh Sachs's *Passionate Intelligence: Imagination and Reason in the Work of Samuel Johnson*; Chester F. Chapin's *The Religious Thought of Samuel Johnson*; James Gray's *Johnson's Sermons: A Study*; Carey McIntosh's *The Choice of Life: Samuel Johnson and the World of Fiction*; Richard B. Schwartz's *Samuel Johnson and the Problem of Evil*; and Robert G. Walker's *Eighteenth-Century Arguments for Immortality and Johnson's* Rasselas. Nicholas Hudson's recent *Samuel Johnson and Eighteenth-Century Thought* is still another noteworthy contribution to scholarship on Johnson the Christian moralist.

The *Dictionary*

For assistance in treating Johnson's *Dictionary*, probably the finest one-person lexicon of English ever compiled, teachers have drawn, according to our questionnaire, on two works, James H. Sledd and Gwin J. Kolb's *Dr. Johnson's* Dictionary: *Essays in the Biography of a Book* and Robert DeMaria's *Johnson's* Dictionary *and the Language of Learning*. To this group should be added Allen Reddick's *The Making of Johnson's* Dictionary, *1746–1773*, which contains much fresh information.

Literary Criticism

Johnson's stature as a literary critic has never been loftier; indeed, some experts believe that he excels all his competitors in English literature. The results of our poll indicate that Jean H. Hagstrum's *Samuel Johnson's Literary Criticism* is considered the most valuable scrutiny of the subject. Two essays, W. R. Keast's "The Theoretical Foundations of Johnson's Criticism" and T. S. Eliot's "Johnson as Critic and Poet," stand out among shorter pieces on the topic. In addition, Damrosch's *Samuel Johnson and the Tragic Sense* and *The Uses of Johnson's Criticism* and William Edinger's *Samuel Johnson and Poetic Style* received commendations for their discerning, stimulating discussions. Of older works, Joseph Epes Brown's *Critical Opinions of Samuel Johnson* and W. B. C. Watkins's *Johnson and English Poetry before 1660* offer much relevant material and numerous insights to the instructor seeking aid in teaching the critical works (and, with respect to Watkins's study, the *Dictionary*).

Biographies

By eighteenth-century specialists, Johnson the biographer is usually ranked second only to Boswell, who, in the opening pages of the *Life*, acknowledges his large indebtedness to the theory and practice that his friend and subject had advanced in *Rambler* no. 60. One book — Robert Folkenflik's pioneering *Samuel Johnson, Biographer* — while concentrating on the *Lives of the Poets*, briefly treats the many biographies, short and substantial, composed by Johnson over a period of more than forty years. But a number of the essays in the collections edited by Hilles (*New Light*), Korshin, and Nath, as well as portions of the books cited by Damrosch (*Uses*) and Grundy (*Scale*), throw much light on individual biographies or groups of biographies. Moreover, the following studies have notably improved my classroom handling of various lives: Bergen B. Evans's "Dr. Johnson's Theory of Biography," Benjamin Boyce's "Johnson's *Life of Savage* and Its Literary Background," and John Butt's *Biography in the Hands of Walton, Johnson, and Boswell*.

Letters

Besides writing probably the best-known individual letter (to the fourth earl of Chesterfield) in English literature, Johnson, of course, is currently eliciting increased recognition as a versatile master of the "great epistolick art." Until an extended treatment of his correspondence appears, we must draw enlightenment from R. W. Chapman's "The Formal Parts of Johnson's Letters"; Grundy's "The Techniques of Spontaneity: Johnson's Developing Epistolary Style"; and Bruce Redford's "Samuel Johnson and Mrs. Thrale: The 'Little Language' of the Public Moralist."

Political Writings and *A Journey to the Western Islands of Scotland*

Like his letters, Johnson's political writings and his travel narrative *A Journey to the Western Islands of Scotland* are now receiving marked scholarly and critical attention. The standard examinations of the first group of pieces are Benjamin B. Hoover's *Samuel Johnson's Parliamentary Reporting* and Greene's *The Politics of Samuel Johnson*. Different opinions of the form and contents of the *Journey* prevent the designation of a single discussion as standard; Thomas M. Curley's expansive *Samuel Johnson and the Age of Travel* devotes a chapter, "Philosophic Art and Travel in the Highlands," to a scrutiny of the "peerless work."

Miscellaneous Publications

Depending on their particular approaches, emphases, and interests, instructors will find these miscellaneous publications worthy helpmates in teaching Johnson: Mary Hyde's *The Thrales of Streatham Park*; John A. Vance's *Samuel Johnson and the Sense of History*; Morris R. Brownell's *Samuel Johnson's Attitude to the Arts*; John Wiltshire's *Samuel Johnson in the Medical World*; *Johnsonian News Letter* (which originated in 1940, appears four times a year, and is edited by Stuart Sherman and issued from the University of Chicago); and *The Age of Johnson: A Scholarly Annual*, containing both articles and reviews (it originated in 1988 and is edited by Paul J. Korshin).

Biographies

Boswell's *Life of Johnson* (the standard edition is that prepared by G. B. Hill and L. F. Powell, 1934-64), for most students the premier biography in the language, obviously merits the pride of place in this section. But Boswell's work should be supplemented by John Hawkins's *Life* (1787); G. B. Hill's edition of *Johnsonian Miscellanies* (2 vols., 1897), which includes, among other pieces, Hester Lynch Thrale Piozzi's *Anecdotes* of Johnson (1786) and Arthur Murphy's essay on Johnson (1792); and, most important, several excellent twentieth-century biographies: Joseph Wood Krutch's *Samuel Johnson*, James L. Clifford's *Young Sam Johnson* and *Dictionary Johnson: Samuel Johnson's Middle Years*, John Wain's *Samuel Johnson*, and Walter Jackson Bate's *Samuel Johnson*.

Furthermore, some teachers may have occasion to consult *Early Biographies of Samuel Johnson*, edited by O M Brack, Jr., and Robert E. Kelley, which includes fourteen brief life stories, and the eleven-volume *Johnsonian Gleanings*, by Aleyn Lyell Reade, a work that sets forth a remarkable succession of significant discoveries about Johnson's life and connected matters. In addition, Thomas Kaminski's *Early Career of Samuel Johnson*, covering the period from 1737 to 1746, and Edward A. Bloom's *Samuel Johnson in Grub Street*, concentrating on the journalistic productions (mostly) from 1738 to 1760, should be read by those who want a detailed treatment of Johnson's development into a professional writer. Finally, W. B. C. Watkins's *Perilous Balance: The Tragic Genius of Swift, Johnson, and Sterne*, Bertrand H. Bronson's "Johnson Agonistes," and George Irwin's *Samuel Johnson: A Personality in Conflict* furnish revealing, suggestive analyses of Johnson's intellectual and psychological makeup.

Background Studies

Heading the group of background studies utilized by our respondents is Donald Greene's *The Age of Exuberance: Backgrounds to Eighteenth-Century English Literature*, which provides an admirable account of the energetic political, social, economic, intellectual, and artistic activities of the period. Other well-regarded works include M. Dorothy George's *London Life in the Eighteenth Century*, *Johnson's England* (ed. Turberville), Basil Willey's *The Eighteenth-Century Background: Studies on the Idea of Nature in the Thought of the Period*, Roy Porter's *English Society of the Eighteenth Century*, Richard B. Schwartz's *Daily Life in Johnson's London*, and James Sambrook's *The Eighteenth Century: The Intellectual and Cultural Context of English Literature, 1700-1789*.

Scholarly Editions

The Yale Edition of the Works of Samuel Johnson has reached thirteen volumes — namely, 1, *Diaries, Prayers, and Annals*, edited by E. L. McAdam, Jr., and Donald Hyde and Mary Hyde; 2, *The* Idler *and the* Adventurer, edited by W. J. Bate, John M. Bullitt, and L. F. Powell; 3–5, *The Rambler*, edited by W. J. Bate and Albrecht B. Strauss; 6, *Poems*, edited by E. L. McAdam, Jr., and George Milne; 7–8, *Johnson on Shakespeare*, edited by Arthur Sherbo, introduction by Bertrand H. Bronson; 9, *A Journey to the Western Islands of Scotland*, edited by Mary Lascelles; 10, *Political Writings*, edited by Donald J. Greene; 14, *Sermons*, edited by Jean H. Hagstrum and James Gray; 15, *A Voyage to Abyssinia*, edited by Joel Gold; and 16, *Rasselas and Other Tales* ("The Vision of Theodore" and "The Fountains"), edited by Gwin J. Kolb. None of the earlier editions of Johnson's works can be labeled scholarly, although several — notably, John Hawkins's edition (1787), and the 1792 version (which contains Murphy's essay on Johnson), and Francis Pearson Walesby's edition (Oxford, 1825) — continue to be examined and cited, especially for works not yet part of the Yale Edition.

Moving to individual works, I name, generally in chronological order, a number of outstanding editions. Once called definitive, *Lives of the English Poets* (ed. Hill, 1905) will be superseded by the corresponding volumes of the Yale Edition; until then, an impressive scholarly achievement, it remains the standard version of the work. Similarly, for the present, Allen T. Hazen's edition of *Samuel Johnson's Prefaces and Dedications* (1937), replete with pertinent facts, is the best repository of a sizable group of the minor compositions. Notwithstanding its appearance in the Yale Edition, Johnson's poetry can still be profitably examined in two other editions that treat some topics and contain some information absent from the Yale volume. The earlier, entitled *The Poems of Samuel Johnson* (1941; 2nd ed., 1974), was prepared by David Nichol Smith and Edward L. McAdam, Jr.; the second, *Samuel Johnson: The Complete English Poems* (1971), by J. D. Fleeman. Bruce Redford has completed the Hyde edition of Johnson's letters; the first three volumes were published in 1991, the last two in 1993. Although less inclusive in its scope than the Yale Edition, J. P. Hardy's edition of *Rasselas* (1968) contains a perceptive introduction, the text of R. W. Chapman's edition (1927) of the tale, and useful notes. Clarence Tracy's edition (1971) of the *Life of Savage* also deserves praise for its informative introduction, sound text (with numerous textual notes), and valuable historical annotation. Last, J. D. Fleeman's edition of *A Journey to the Western Islands of Scotland* (1985) far exceeds the Yale Edition in its detailed treatment of textual matters and its splendid commentary and appendixes on a variety of related topics. Eventually, a critical edition of Johnson's *Dictionary* will be produced; while awaiting that happy event, everyone without access to the first (1755) and fourth, heavily revised edition (1773) can use photographic reproductions of both — the first appeared in 1968 (Olms), 1983 (Yoshudo), and 1990 (Longman); the fourth in 1978 (Librairie du Liban). Another reproduction, advertised as a facsimile of the first edition and issued in 1967 and 1979, contains sheets of the first and second editions (1755–56).

Literary Histories

No comprehensive or partial literary history emerged as the leader in the responses to our questionnaire, but all of the following rated positive mentions: M. H. Abrams's *The Mirror and the Lamp: Romantic Theory and the Critical Tradition*, Martin Price's *To the Palace of Wisdom: Studies in Order and Energy from Dryden to Blake*, George Sherburn and Donald F. Bond's *The Restoration and Eighteenth Century*, John Butt and Geoffrey Carnall's *The Mid-Eighteenth Century*, and Maximillian E. Novak's *Eighteenth-Century English Literature*.

Bibliographies

No satisfactory bibliography of Johnson's writings exists, but J. D. Fleeman, of Pembroke College, Oxford, is preparing such a work, which will certainly realize high standards of comprehensiveness and accuracy. Until Fleeman's work appears, we must rely on William P. Courtney and David Nichol Smith's *Bibliography of Samuel Johnson* (1915; reissued in 1925 with illustrations) and R. W. Chapman and Allen T. Hazen's "Johnsonian Bibliography: A Supplement to Courtney" (1939). Despite serious weaknesses, the book and the article, taken together, contain a wealth of useful information. Although limited in scope, the entry on Johnson in the second volume of George Watson and I. R. Willison's *New Cambridge Bibliography of English Literature* also provides adequate answers to many questions. And Fleeman's *Preliminary Handlist of Documents and Manuscripts of Samuel Johnson* (1967) serves admirably the needs of those wishing knowledge about nonprinted materials.

Turning from mostly primary to mostly secondary materials, I place first two indispensable compilations, James L. Clifford and Donald J. Greene's *Samuel Johnson: A Survey and Bibliography of Critical Studies* and Greene and John A. Vance's *Bibliography of Johnsonian Studies, 1970–1985*, which record (under 25 separate headings) virtually all significant scholarship on Johnson's life and writings through 1985, list reviews of much of this scholarship, and indicate — through the use of asterisks — the items judged most important by the compilers. Another helpful resource is *The Eighteenth Century: A Current Bibliography*, covering numerous disciplines, languages, and countries, now an independent work but appearing annually in *Philology Quarterly* from 1971 through 1975. *The Eighteenth Century* succeeds the narrower "English Literature, 1660–1800: A Current Bibliography," founded by Ronald S. Crane and published yearly in *Philological Quarterly* from 1926 through 1970 (the entire series was also photographed and issued in six volumes — 1 [1950], 2 [1952], 3–4 [1962], 5–6 [1972] — by Princeton University Press). Both the original bibliography and the expanded version contain many, often searching, reviews of selected articles and books. Last, readers should be reminded of volume 1 (including the "British Isles" and, of course, a section on Johnson) of the annual *MLA International Bibliography of Books and Articles on the Modern Languages and Literatures*, which began in 1922 as a section (entitled "American Bibliography" and limited to American scholarship) of *PMLA*.

Nonprinted Materials

Besides the printed materials noted above, tapes of eighteenth-century music (particularly, compositions by Handel, Mozart, and Haydn) have been suggested as effective supplements to classroom presentations of Johnson's works (probably his last prose piece was the dedication, to George III, of Charles Burney's *Account of the Commemoration of Handel*, 1785). And one respondent recommended the showing of the Yale University Films videotape *Boswell's London Journal*, which includes the famous first meeting between Johnson and Boswell.

Part Two

APPROACHES

GENERAL APPROACHES

Samuel Johnson and Gender

Catherine N. Parke

> Too much is made of Dr. Johnson on women preachers
> and not enough of his support of Fanny Burney.
> — Jane Marcus,
> *Art and Anger: Reading like a Woman*

In the contemporary climate of critical theory and practice, gender studies and the several feminisms are generally understood to be, by teachers and students alike, legitimate and useful perspectives on literature. It now nearly goes without saying that considerations of gender (its politics, history, and ideology), my subject in this essay, are a regular part of our classroom business.

To read from the perspective of gender means to consider how the socially defined portraiture to which we give the names *man* and *woman* functions in the creation, production, and reception of literature. This proposition about the social construction of gender is one of the central tenets of post-structuralist critical theory and practice. Some of the notorious statements attributed to Samuel Johnson, such as the remark cited in Boswell's *Life*, "Sir, a woman's preaching is like a dog's walking on his hinder legs. It is not done well; but you are surprized to find it done at all" (1: 463, ed. Hill and Powell) — a statement that, unhappily, students have often encountered before reading a word written by Johnson himself — seem to invite particular scrutiny on the subject of gender. In my teaching I do not discuss Johnson and his writings exclusively or even predominantly in terms of gender. Yet over the past six or seven years of my eighteen years in the classroom, issues of gender have increasingly influenced the ways both I and my students read.

My aim in this essay, as in the classroom, is neither simply to condemn nor to acquit Johnson on charges of sexism. His political correctness, as such, is not my topic, although a verdict on this subject is almost inevitably a by-product of such discussion. Rather, my aim is the more encompassing one of offering some terms for a more ranging and fruitful discussion of Johnson that identifies aspects of his work and of the historical transmission of his image that might otherwise be overlooked or considered unimportant. This discussion sheds light equally on Johnson himself, on his writings, and on us his audience. It leads to productive examinations of what constitutes evidence and the rules of evidence in literary study, of how one determines what is present and what is not in a literary text, of how society constructs its categories of the natural and the normal and translates them into literature, among other forms, in order to organize and prompt certain kinds of behavior on the part of its members. In this essay, I first discuss gender and Johnson "the man," then apply considerations of gender to a sampling of his work, and finally locate Johnson in the context of the onset of neoconservatism in the last quarter of the eighteenth century. My remarks are drawn from experiences of teaching two courses on the later eighteenth century, one an upper-level undergraduate survey of the period and the other a graduate seminar. My students have played no small part in contributing to my ideas on Johnson and gender.

In "The Double Tradition of Dr. Johnson," Bertrand H. Bronson observes that "a great writer is defined not only by his own works but also by what posterity makes of him." Bronson continues: "After his death there springs up an eidolon of an author, and it is of this everchanging surrogate, not of the original, that we inevitably form our judgements, and that by so judging we further change" (90). If there were no readers, writers might remain original and pure. But if writers retain any reputation, and since even an uncomplimentary reputation is probably preferable to none at all, generations of readers subsequently make of authors what they will and thus keep those authors current.

Certain writers more than others become powerfully and hence often prejudicially part of the very cultural air we breathe. Johnson is one of these, and Gertrude Stein, Sigmund Freud, and Virginia Woolf are among the better known others. Students often "know" these writers as part of our cultural mythos without having read a word of their works. Stein, for instance, is familiar from her famous repetition "a rose is a rose is a rose is a rose." Most students have heard of Freud's primal scene and Oedipus complex. They also usually have some idea, if an unsophisticated one, that his thinking about women is problematic. Students often vaguely associate Woolf with *Who's Afraid of Virginia Woolf?* though they rarely recognize it to be the title of a play by Edward Albee. It makes less sense, I think, and is certainly less interesting to attribute this kind of acquaintance to students' mere

laziness or fuzzy thinking than to see it as testimony to the continuing promi-
nence, however unexamined or erroneous, of Stein, Freud, and Woolf in
our cultural imagination. Their eidolons are no less real for being sometimes
superficial and sometimes specious.

The Johnson whom students know before they take an eighteenth-century
course is usually in some fashion, however attenuated, Boswell's Johnson.
This is also the Johnson who seems ready at hand when a journalist, inter-
viewer, or editorial writer needs a quotable conservative to pillory. In my
unsystematic and admittedly partial survey over the years, I have encountered more than once the following Johnsonisms in the popular media and
occasionally in more self-announcedly literary writing: "Consider, of what
importance to society the chastity of women is. Upon that all the property
in the world depends" (Boswell, *Life* 5: 209); "The woman's a whore, and
there's an end on't" (2: 247); "Sir, your wife, *under pretence of keeping
a bawdy-house*, is a receiver of stolen goods" (4: 26); and the perennial quote
about the woman preacher memorialized most damningly in Adrienne Rich's
poem "Snapshots of a Daughter-in-Law" *"Not that it is done well, but /
that it is done at all?* Yes, think / of the odds! or shrug them off forever"
(38). How can we know for sure how to read such comments, even supposing
them to be, word for word, Johnson's own? What was their tone or tones?
On what evidence do we base our interpretations?

In her memoirs of Johnson, Frances Reynolds says how much she wishes
"in justice to Dr. Johnson's character, that the many jocular and ironical
speeches which have been recorded of him had been mark'd as such, for
the information of those who were unacquainted with him" (Hill, *Johnsonian Miscellanies* 2: 271). Her wish aptly directs us to imagine various
possibilities for the speaker's inflections and to adopt a healthy skepticism
about any unitary, certain, or exclusive reading of these popular sayings.
Otherwise we risk unworthily making Johnson a scapegoat for our own complacency, superiority, and unconscious insecurities.

While remarks that, on the face of them, might make Johnson out to be
a good old boy appear frequently, other comments attributed to him that
would be more explicitly congenial to current notions of politically correct
attitudes toward gender appear rarely: "No woman is the worse for sense and
knowledge" (Boswell, *Life* 5: 226); or "Men know that women are an over-
match for them, and therefore they choose the weakest or most ignorant.
If they did not think so, they never could be afraid of women knowing as
much as themselves" (5: 226); or "I had often wondered why young women
should marry, as they have so much more freedom, and so much more attention paid to them while unmarried, than when married" (2: 471). This
speaker is still Boswell's Johnson rather than Johnson in his own written
words. But the figure depicted in these utterances seems to be not a carica-
turishly unenlightened conservative but instead an astute and progressive
observer of his culture.

The Johnson whom students think they know is, then, often a kind of historical barometer who registers the prejudices we all, in more or less sophisticated ways, instinctively feel toward the past. The belief that our own times have improved on the past is perhaps synonymous with life itself and with the natural, though not always accurate or worthy, urge to make a place for ourselves by supplanting our predecessors. Students are likely to believe that writers who lived "back then" or in "those times," phrases I often hear, were backward in everything from intelligence to politics to sexual attitudes and practice. Thus for Johnson, as for all the writers I teach, not just in eighteenth-century courses, I always ask the students to jot down what they know about the authors we are about to read before we begin our study of them. This exercise helps students see that, by college age, they have ideas and opinions, sometimes conscious, sometimes unconscious, on all manner of subjects. I ask the class to repeat this exercise fifteen weeks later, at the end of the term. Invariably students have forgotten their first answers and are genuinely surprised when they compare their before-and-after sketches. Far from being a mere pep rally for dead writers, this exercise provides a formal occasion to think about what it means to become acquainted with figures from the past and to recognize and reckon with the parochialism of uncritically favoring the present.

Since our attitudes toward the past often say as much about us as about that imagined time, there is clearly more at stake in examining Johnson's opinions about men and women than a mere cross-examination of him on possible charges of sexism. Indeed, an examination of his popular reputation, of which his attitudes about gender constitute a part, educates us about the history of his reception and the construction of his image. Consider for instance, that, by 1800, sixteen years after his death, seventeen biographies had appeared. Biographies are always significant testimony to their subjects' popularity, a measure of the interest that biographers and publishers alike imagine already to exist or to be readily evoked in the reading public. It is surely no accident that two of Johnson's most notable contemporary biographers were a man and a woman—namely, James Boswell and Hester Lynch Thrale Piozzi. His friends in life, they competed for the reading public's interest, belief, and allegiance in their biographies after his death. Boswell's *Life* and Piozzi's *Anecdotes* make a fascinating pair for class discussion in no small part because the works raise issues of gender in several interconnected ways relating to the complexities of friendship and antagonism, to the mystery of creativity, and to the imaginative construction of other people's lives. These two writers' distinct points of view, their cognitive and emotional attitudes toward Johnson, would seem to be inextricably bound up with, among other qualities, their genders. Each knew Johnson in a way the other did not, at least in part because he apparently talked to these two friends differently, as their differences of character, mind, temperament, and gender would hardly make surprising. (For an intriguing analysis of the seeming contradictions of these two accounts, see Hyde's *The Impossible Friendship: Boswell and Mrs. Thrale.*)

Thrale was woman, wife, and mother. She was apparently, on balance, nurturing, patient, solicitous, bright, and, at least outwardly, cheerful. Boswell was, when Johnson first met him, a young man about town, later a husband, father, and lawyer. He was alternately melancholy and ebullient, unreliable, dependent, inventive, and self-indulgent. To Boswell, Johnson was a surrogate father who combined encouragement with love and tutorial discipline in equal parts. With Thrale, Johnson was, by turns, childlike, fatherlike, and suitorlike, his behavior ranging from the confessional to the demanding, the brusque to the affectionate. Their two accounts portray different, though interrelated, aspects of the man's makeup. Boswell's multi-volume work contrasts with Thrale's slim, pocketable book, the difference in size implying different assertions of authority by each writer — assertions conventionally associated with their genders.

In our own period, most notably over the past fifteen years, Johnson scholars and critics have made substantial and illuminating inquiries into Johnson's attitudes and behavior toward women in his life and writings. Among the most noteworthy are a study of Johnson as literary patron of four important women writers (Elizabeth Carter, Charlotte Lennox, Frances Burney, and Hannah More), by Gae Brack; an inquiry into his encouragement of women to become patrons of other women, by Isobel Grundy; a feminist reading of *Rasselas* by Marlene Hansen, who argues its fundamentally egalitarian presentation of men and women; studies of Johnson's increasingly enlightened images of women throughout his writing career and of his analysis of prostitution as a socioeconomic ill rather than as a female moral failure, by Sheryl Rae O'Donnell and by Chella Courington Livingston; an examination of his attitudes on women's education, by Charmaine Wellington; reinterpretations of his relationship with Thrale, by Martine Watson Brownley and by John C. Riely; an account of his three most intimate relations with women (his mother, his wife, and Thrale) and of his other friendships with many different women, by Margaret Lane. To this significant pattern of female friendships and empowering associations during his lifetime — summarized by Frances Reynolds in her observation that he "set a higher value upon female friendship than, perhaps, most men" (Hill, *Johnsonian Miscellanies* 2: 252) — might be added the legacy of subsequent notable women writers who turned what they learned from his work to their own distinctive purposes — Jane Austen, Virginia Woolf, and Gertrude Stein, among them.

This recent reassessment of Johnson by women scholars and critics is the modern-day equivalent of Johnson's many friendships with women in his own day. Cumulatively this scholarship depicts a man whose attitude toward women was, at the very least, "in general benign and rather enlightened" (Rogers 9). Thus in its reappraisal of Johnson on gender issues and its reemphasis on his writings, twentieth-century criticism has come full circle to a view of the man more in keeping with that of his contemporaries.

I now turn from this brief examination of Johnson the man and the transmission of his image in relation to gender to a consideration of some of his writings, which he himself would have preferred to be judged by. For the balance of the nineteenth century, his writings were overlooked in favor of Johnson the man and, particularly, the conversationalist, a more palatable and interesting figure for several generations of readers. The twentieth century has redressed this imbalance while retaining an avid interest in Johnson the man. Among the writings that I have found most readily to invite and, in turn, to be enlightened by discussions of gender are the *Rambler*, *Life of Savage*, *Irene*, and *Rasselas*.

For a discussion of the *Rambler* essays, I begin by noting Johnson's definitions of *man* and *woman* in the *Dictionary* (1755). Among the fourteen definitions of *man* are "a human being" and "any one," while the two definitions of *woman* are "the female of the human race" and "a female attendant on a person of rank." *Woman* is thus the marked term, and one may arguably assume that all the essays, unless specified as being about women, include both sexes. By my count some 27 out of a total of 208 essays are specifically about women; of these, 15 use a female persona. These essays range from the comedy of petty complaints by vapid women who are bored during the summer season (no. 124) to the outrage and suffering inflicted on Misella, who is betrayed by a relative and led into prostitution (nos. 170 and 171). Implicit throughout the *Rambler* and explicitly foregrounded in such essays as no. 149, on the psychological abuse of children, is Johnson's unconditional and gender-blind opposition to abuses of power. This overarching principle, in turn, directs his considerations of gender politics.

The *Life of Savage* (1744) is an explicitly gender-focused narrative. It depicts a cruel and unnatural mother, Anne, the countess of Macclesfield, whose self-proclaimed bastard son (on Johnson's error in genealogy, see Tracy's edition), Richard Savage, is Johnson's sympathetic as well as cautionary subject. Johnson partially explains, if not excuses, the son's wasted genius and self-destructiveness in terms of his mother's abandonment and refusal either to help or to acknowledge him. Her behavior, in Johnson's estimation, amounted to active harm against her offspring. Johnson depicts the countess as the bad mother and the unchaste woman, the two types linked in caricaturish yet still powerful ways with a long tradition in Western literature. It is curious that Johnson, a man devoted to truth, chose to believe Savage's account of the countess, apparently without verifying the story. His credulousness inevitably raises questions about the force of cultural stereotype even in a writer as intelligent as Johnson and about his own

Freudian family romance that may have contributed to his susceptibility to Savage's account (Gross 48–54).

Irene (1749), Johnson's verse tragedy, combines the tradition of the "she-tragedy," which centers on a woman in distress and features a heightened emphasis on pathos, with the new popular interest in exotic lands. The author created two distressed women, Irene and her friend Aspasia, two Greek Christian captives of the invading Turkish commander Mahomet. Irene sacrifices her religion and her virtue for the wealth and power promised by Mahomet. The virtuous Aspasia tries to save her friend from ruin by arguing the importance of female patience, modesty, and piety.

To dramatize this story of temptation, appetite, and virtue, Johnson wrote speeches for his three principal characters that summarize the main opposing positions in the eighteenth-century debate on woman's nature. Making a radical critique of the social system, Aspasia observes that women are weak because they are corruptly educated: "Instructed from our infant years to court / With counterfeited fears the aid of man" (*Poems*, 2.1.27–28, ed. McAdam and Milne). Mahomet, the tyrannical, lustful, and misogynistic foreigner, argues that women's "inferiour natures" are "form'd to delight, and happy by delighting" (2.7.16). Irene, meanwhile, attempts to reason with her captor and would-be lover on the nature of woman's soul, fairer in proportion to her beauty than man's. She also asks the unspeakable question, "Beats not the female breast with gen'rous passions, / The thirst of empire, and the love of glory?" (2.7.57–58). Aspasia, in some ways arguably the quintessential womanly woman, though no mere stereotype of female submission, opposes Irene's emphasis on women's equal appetite for fame and fortune, asserting that heaven "[m]ade passive fortitude the praise of woman" (3.8.44). Predictably, Irene suffers the consequences of her pride, ambition, and apostasy. The play elaborates and exploits gender divisions along an axis that plots passion, the uncontrolled urge for power, and the self-betrayal of one's gender against self-control, patriotism, and the "natural" acting out of gender.

In *Rasselas* (1759), by contrast, women and men characters are virtually indistinguishable. The story recounts the adventures of Prince Rasselas, Princess Nekayah, and the Lady Pekuah, who, along with their teacher Imlac, escape from the happy valley in order to see the world and find the happy choice of life. Gender, sexuality, and their attendant passions appear only briefly in the tale, in three episodes serving as monitory examples of the improper italicizing of gender: Nekayah's inquiry into family life and the miseducation of daughters (91–92, ed. Kolb), Pekuah's kidnapping, and her account of the boring, empty lives of women in her Arab kidnapper's seraglio (138–40). The Arab chief values Pekuah primarily for her intelligent attention to his astronomy lessons. He does not exploit her physically as a sexual object, but his selfish interest in her silent attention to his celestial observations is condescending, and his holding her against her will is criminal.

The closest Johnson comes to gender stereotyping occurs in the conclusion (175–76), in which the young characters express their ideal wishes. Pekuah wants to become a prioress, Nekayah to found a college for women, and Rasselas to govern his kingdom. In choosing education and the religious life, these young women, one might say, select conventionally female work. Yet surely it is significant that neither expresses the wish to marry and that both imagine their futures in terms of vocation.

On balance, then, the relations among all the characters, within and across gender lines, emphasize friendship and virtual equality. As one critic remarks, "In avoiding romance and eroticism and instead emphasizing friendship in this way, Johnson manages to avoid the polarization of the sexes" (Hansen 522). The two principal women in *Rasselas* are virtually indistinguishable from the men in language, thought, and feelings, and vice versa. From the outset, the women are taken seriously. Their gender is never in any sense made to seem a liability to the group's journey.

In writing a tale about education and the attainment of the greater wisdom that constitutes healthy human relations and earthly happiness, Johnson minimized passion and hence sexual difference in order to emphasize his firmly held belief that education is synonymous with freedom and that it knows no gender bounds. Correlatively, he despised Milton for his hypocrisy in being a republican, on the one hand, and a man contemptuous of women, on the other: "There appears in his books something like a Turkish contempt of females, as subordinate and inferior beings. That his own daughters might not break the ranks, he suffered them to be depressed by a mean and penurious education. He thought woman made only for obedience, and man only for rebellion" (*Lives* 1: 157, ed. Hill). Johnson's repugnance at the discrepancy between Milton's political attitudes and his behavior is deeply felt and powerfully expressed.

In his fundamentally gender-democratic attitudes toward education, Johnson joins, perhaps most notably, Mary Wollstonecraft, whose life overlaps the last twenty-five years of his. Her most famous and influential essay, *A Vindication of the Rights of Woman* (1792), appeared eight years after Johnson's death. This defense of equal education for men and women identifies as its chief antagonists Jean-Jacques Rousseau, whose neoprimitivism and high valuing of sensibility Johnson abhorred, and John Gregory, cleric and author of the popular *Father's Legacy to His Daughter* (1774), an essay instructing young women that their first duty is to please men. These men defined woman's chief duty as living completely for others by combining perfect charm with perfect virtue. The two writers express and typify neoconservative, middle-class fears that were on the rise during the last quarter of the eighteenth century: Rousseau with his emphasis on womanly submissiveness and charm; Gregory with his exhortation to young women to keep their learning "a profound secret, especially from men" (31).

The fears that, in turn, led to Rousseau's and Gregory's popularity in England arose in reaction to the American and French Revolutions combined with increasing economic and political discontent at home. The last years of the eighteenth century, following Johnson's death, and the early years of the next century were a complex and self-contradictory time during which women lost more than they gained. As one who, by reasons of temperament and personal history, identified with the oppressed, Johnson knew that such groups would eventually rise up against their oppressors, and rightly so. He would not have been surprised by the nineteenth-century women's movement, though undoubtedly he would have regretted the need for it.

The historian Joan Kelly observes that when we look at "ages or movements of great social change in terms of their liberation or repression of woman's potential . . . what emerges is a fairly regular pattern of relative loss of status for women precisely in those periods of so-called progressive change" (2). In the last years of Johnson's life, middle-class England was settling into an antirevolutionary period of right-wing backlash that extended well into the next century (Lorch 102). Seen against this backdrop, his lack of condescension toward and active support of women in both his life and his writings invite a second look. This behavior raises issues that, far from commending our self-satisfaction about living in a thoroughly improved age, cross-examine our complacency and return us to Johnson with fresh eyes.[1]

NOTE

[1] A version of this essay first appeared in *South Central Review* 9 (1992): 71–80. Reprinted with permission.

Resisting Authority; or, Johnson
and the Wizard of Oz

James G. Basker

Samuel Johnson may be the single most imposing, authoritative figure in the whole tradition of English literature, a reputation that does nothing to endear him to students in the late twentieth century—or to their teachers, for that matter. Consider the titles that generations of critics have laid on him over the past two hundred years: "Literary Dictator," "the Colossus of Literature," "Ursa Major," "the Great Cham [Khan or Ruler] of Litera-ture," "Johnson Agonistes," "Dictionary Johnson"—rarely anything more informal or inviting than "Doctor Johnson," a title with power to intimidate even today when doctoral degrees are so common. As Frederick Bogel aptly observes, the phrase "*Johnsonian authority* is nearly a redundancy" (189).

Of the many kinds of literary works with which we associate Johnson, the two that have had the most lasting influence over the shape of literary culture are precisely the two that loom with greatest authority in the lives of today's students: the dictionary and the literary anthology (the latter often interchangeable with "textbook"). To the authority of these texts over their language, their thought and expression, even their imaginative horizons, we ask or allow millions of students to subject themselves every year. No wonder teachers and students have not rushed to develop classes based on Johnson's *Dictionary of the English Language* (1755) and his *Lives of the Poets* (1779–81) and their consequences for literature and society today.

Yet it is through these two classic works, pillars of our cultural heritage and arguably Johnson's most influential publications, that we can present students with some of the most unconventional, irreverent, and provocative ideas about literature. Students learn that to ignore historic institutions and inherited forms is to acquiesce blindly in their authority. They may also find, as other subjects have, that deconstructing authority can be exhilarating. Through these two texts students can come not only to see and enjoy the irreverent, subversive side of Johnson—Johnson the bad boy—but also to learn ways to understand better all the "texts" in their lives, from school-books to videos, clothing, and every other kind of cultural construct. They can see that while order and authority are necessary in our world, all authority is to some degree like the voice over the loudspeaker or the Wizard of Oz behind the curtain: obeyed because invisible, imperative, and unques-tioned. My approach to teaching Johnson's *Dictionary* and *Lives of the Poets* rests on three basic principles: (1) *historical knowledge* of how the texts were actually written, in what circumstances and for what audience; (2) *close reading* of passages in the texts themselves; and (3) *experiential learning*, in which the students reenact the process of production or compilation to pro-duce their own versions of similar texts. It is the last of these that ultimately makes the other two effective, but I should outline the first two before moving on to specific examples of assignments and projects that shape the core of the students' learning experience.

Historical knowledge about the actual composition of these two works is necessary to clear away the heavy accretions of misinformation and misconception. Both are in a sense "displaced texts." The *Dictionary* represents two hundred years of attention focused on what is essentially the wrong book. Johnson's massive folio edition of the *Dictionary* — its detailed entries replete with etymologies, usage labels, Johnsonian comments and speculations, and thousands of supportive quotations from major writers and experts — was unknown to the vast majority of readers. What they read was the abridged edition, one-tenth the size, one-fifteenth the price, one hundred times more numerous but also infinitely more cryptic, impersonal, and authoritarian. Compared with the folio, it is a petty dictator of a text. It is this form that has fostered what one scholar calls "the Anglo-American tradition of dictionary worship" (McDavid xx) and left us with the passivity evident in our habitual phraseology: Look it up in the dictionary or Is it in the dictionary? but almost never Is the dictionary correct? Is it complete? What has been left out? Does it agree with the ways I hear and read the word used in society? Who wrote it? or Who says so?

With the *Lives of the Poets*, the displacement is different but equally telling. The *Lives* are the correct texts to read, but they are lumped together under a wrong and misleading title, detached from their original setting and purpose, and claimed as proper subject matter by exactly the wrong crowd of readers (that is, by scholars and academic critics rather than the great mass of general readers for whom they were intended, Johnson's "common readers"). When students learn the true story of how Johnson was commissioned for a large fee to write *Prefaces, Biographical and Critical* for the sections of a commercial anthology, how his publishers were paying for his prestigious name as much as his expertise, how he had almost no say in the selection of poets and works included in that anthology, and how he wrote those prefaces with a general and not a scholarly audience in mind (Bate, *Samuel Johnson* 525–46), they quickly begin to rethink their approach to *all* anthologies and textbooks, to question how and why and with what aims and under whose sponsorship similar books came into being. In short, the issue of canonicity becomes a reality.

In this context, close reading takes on new meaning. When students are asked to read critically the text of a dictionary or of an anthology preface — works they are used to thinking of as informational, not imaginative or aesthetic — they are uncomfortable at first. But armed with knowledge about the history of the texts, they become better close readers, alert to shifts, omissions, a whole array of rhetorical structures and strategies, and their possible implications.

The key to "reading" Johnson's *Dictionary* is to juxtapose entries for the same word from the unabridged and the abridged editions. (Selected excerpts will serve in place of the dictionaries themselves, which can be very expensive even in facsimile.) In contrasting the cryptic entries of the abridgment with the much more detailed and yet also more ambiguous and provisional entries of the unabridged edition, students can see how much has been omitted and suppressed. Not just the text itself but the fundamental relation between reader and text has been radically transformed. The abridgment, one discovers, subjects the reader to a seemingly arbitrary and unquestionable authority. Thus in the unabridged edition, under the verb *to knuckle*, Johnson sounds uncertain, openly speculative, and anything but dictatorial:

> To submit: I suppose from an odd custom of striking the under side of the table with the knuckles, in confession of an argumental defeat.

Contrast this with the clipped certitude of the abridgment:

> *To knuckle*: To submit.

This pattern is repeated ad infinitum. In the folio edition, Johnson admits ignorance (e.g., under *kidney*, "Etymology unknown"); presents contradictory opinions from other authorities (e.g., under *zany*, "Probably of *zanei*, the contraction of Giovanni [or] from *sanna*, a scoff, according to Skinner"); introduces and even cultivates ambiguity (e.g., for *cyprus*, a kind of fabric, "I suppose from the place where it was made; or corruptly from *cypress*, as being used in mourning"); and interjects personal comments and occasional jokes (as in his famous entries for *grubstreet*, *lexicographer*, *oats*, etc.). All this textual luxuriousness and openness disappears from the abridged editions.

Most important, in his lavish use of quotations Johnson had made his folio *Dictionary* a reader-friendly text. Everywhere there are serendipitous pleasures and benefits for the reader. The quotations give it the qualities of encyclopedia, book of maxims, and collection of poetic beauties all in one. And the quotations present a standing invitation to readers to enter in and make their own judgments, as in this entry for *knavery*:

> 2. Mischievous tricks or practices. In the following passage it seems a general term for anything put to an ill use, or perhaps of trifling things of more cost than use.
>
> We'll revel it as bravely as the best. With amber bracelets, beads, and all this *knav'ry*.   Shakespeare

In the abridgment, all these speculative comments are stripped away:

> *Knavery*. 2. Mischievous tricks or practices. Shakespeare.

The spareness of the entries gives the text of the abridgment an authoritarian severity. It shuts readers out, subjects them to an invisible and impersonal authority, and reduces authors like Shakespeare to mere totems invoked to enforce strict little definitions. And who among us was not brought up on abridged dictionaries? Indeed, who among the general reading public ever uses anything else? To read Johnson's original text against that of an abridged edition (there were scores of them) is to pierce the veil of authority, to connect the booming voice of Oz with the frantic little man behind the curtain and to begin to address all that such imposture implies.

Similarly, one way to make students confident about approaching any or all of Johnson's *Prefaces, Biographical and Critical* (*The Lives of the Poets*) is to give them three basic reading keys. The first is contextual. As Johnson was writing the prefaces for a mass-market anthology, his primary purpose was to introduce ordinary readers to the works and to prepare them to read the poems for themselves — and not, as so many critics have seemed to assume, to make critical pronouncements ex cathedra. Careful readers will even find rhetorical gestures in the text (e.g., "I must therefore recommend the perusal of his work" — Cowley) made as if the poems were at hand, as indeed they once were (*Lives* 1: 10, ed. Rhys). As for the composition of his readership, Johnson obviously assumed such diversity that it would include students and novice readers about to read these poets' works for the first time (e.g., warning of the diction in Milton's major works "that an unlearned reader, when he first opens his book, finds himself surprised by a new language" [1: 111]).

With this corrected sense of audience and purpose, two other recurrent features become keys to reading Johnson's rhetoric. One is what I call the biographical hook — an anecdote, or personality flaw, or wry comment by Johnson that appears near the beginning of each preface and serves at once to engage the readers' attention, to draw them into reading more about a literary figure whose life suddenly seems less venerable, more curious, more human than ordinary readers might have expected. Of course Johnson placed the biography at the beginning of each of the prefaces because he believed, as he wrote in *Idler* no. 84, that "biography is, of the various kinds of narrative writing, that which is most eagerly read, and most easily applied to the purposes of life." But perhaps sensing that readers might expect less of interest in the lives of poets, and especially that to perform the seemingly obligatory reading of an anthology preface, they might come unenthusiastically to the task, Johnson contrives to lead with a piece of what he and the editors of today's popular press would recognize as human interest.

Thus in the first few lines of their respective prefaces, we learn that Watts's father was a shoemaker, Collins's a hatter, and Akenside's a butcher; also that Broome was born "of very mean parents," that Milton's father had been disinherited, and that Pope was strangely evasive about his father because, says Johnson, he was "more willing . . . to show what his father was not, than what he was" (2: 275, 143). Childhood oddities abound. Watts started Latin at age four; Addison was so puny and feeble at birth that he was christened the same day; Thomson wrote poems as a child but burned them every New Year's Day; Phillips was a teacher's pet who also had a fetish for having his hair combed.

Many of the anecdotes debunk intellectual reputations. Addison was a prankster at school who led the boys in "barring out" the master; Halifax was a slow student, and Johnson notes wryly that it was none too soon when he left to enter university "for he was already a school-boy of one-and-twenty" (1: 307). Meanwhile, Milton, Smith, Fenton, Otway, and Collins were thrown out of the university or left without finishing, all under suspicious circumstances, and Butler, despite the claims of his relatives, is suspected of never having gone at all.

Johnson shows these literary lions, one after another, to have very human weaknesses. Rochester, despite accounts of his heroism in battle, later earned a reputation "for slinking away in street quarrels" (1: 127). Johnson reports that Denham was in his youth "more given to cards and dice than study," that Pomfret preferred "the company of a mistress" to that of his wife, and that several of the poets had drinking problems, although Parnell at least is to be pitied because his alcoholism was brought on by "the untimely death of a darling son" (1: 47, 265, 312). Beyond grabbing the readers' attention, these biographical hooks invite readers to identify with the poets on a human level and to bring that empathy to bear when they begin to examine their works.

The other reading key concerns Johnson's penchant for outrageous remarks in the critical section of each preface. If we remind ourselves that Johnson was writing not for critics but for the variegated mass of common readers, and if we consider for a moment that some of his remarks are phrased in terms too outrageous even to begin to persuade rather than to provoke, then we must think again how to interpret such comments as these:

Of Congreve's *Incognita*: "I would rather praise it than read it" (2: 2).

Of Thomson's poem "Liberty": "When it first appeared, I tried to read [it], and soon desisted. I have never tried again, and therefore will not hazard either praise or censure" (2: 292).

Of Collins's poetry: "He puts his words out of the common order, seeming to think, with some later candidates for fame, that not to write prose is certainly to write poetry" (2: 316).

And, most notorious, of Milton's *Lycidas*: "Surely no man could have fancied that he read *Lycidas* with pleasure had he not known its author"; and of *Paradise Lost*: "[O]ne of the books which the reader admires and lays down and forgets to take up again. None ever wished it longer than it is" (1: 96, 108).

This style is far from the encomiastic or euphemistic one associated with anthology editors. For ordinary readers, whether coming in reverence or passivity or just ignorance to what they can only assume Johnson has sanctioned as *the* standard collection of English poets, such irreverence is disorienting, and deliberately so. It is what I call tactical iconoclasm. Which of us could read such remarks in the prefaces to an anthology today and remain complacent? What student could feel confident that he or she knew the "correct" line to take on the poet under discussion? Who wouldn't turn to the poems with special attention, whether to defend them from Johnson's startling opinions or, emboldened by his example, to articulate one's own honest response, no matter how eccentric? Here he is, ever the teacher, rousing his students. Here is Johnson himself pulling the curtain on authority, forcing readers to exert themselves and, as with Dorothy and her companions in Oz, to develop the talents latent within them.

From these critical ideas, many specific teaching techniques suggest themselves. Because, to the uninitiated, these texts can seem particularly intimidating, experiential hands-on approaches can help students feel that they have a point of access, a place to start. And because dictionaries and anthologies are universally familiar, students can plunge right in with active assignments that accompany, or even precede, the readings. In teaching these works in both high school and college classes over the past several years, I have found that students respond well to variations of such exercises as the following:

On the *Dictionary*

1. Compile a Ten Most Distorted or a Ten Most Dictatorial list, by comparing Johnson's abridged and unabridged dictionaries to find entries that, as a result of abridgment, seem most radically altered or seem to suppress the most uncertainty, contradiction, or personality.

2. Individually or as a class, compile from the quotations in Johnson's unabridged *Dictionary* a book of maxims or a collection of favorite poetic pieces; or sift through to compare how, and how frequently, favorite individual poets are used. By contrast, count "totems" (mere mentions of authors' names) in the abridgment and analyze the implied hierarchy of this pantheon of poets.

3. Compile a class dictionary using Johnson's method: read approved authors for exemplary usages of words, collect and compare these quotations, select the most useful or illustrious, research etymologies, decide parts of speech, write definitions, attach admonitions on preferred usage; then collate, publish, and discuss or defend the results. (For an added sense of mastering or harnessing Johnson's authority, draw all quotations from his creative works.)

4. Focus on cultural authority (where centered, how exerted) by compiling a class dictionary of slang: develop a list of your own words, find supportive quotations from authorities you accept, use class discussion to decide on definitions, speculate on etymologies, and comment on "proper" usage.

On the *Prefaces, Biographical and Critical*

1. Compile an alternative anthology. [Using Lonsdale's landmark edition of *The New Oxford Book of Eighteenth-Century Verse*, my Barnard students compile their own anthology every year by finding a poem that is not included in Lonsdale, writing a critical or biographical preface that makes the case for including it in a future edition, and then collecting their poems and prefaces into a volume that goes on reserve as a reading for the course.]

2. Compile an anthology de novo in virtually any field of literature, establishing editorial criteria, selecting and writing prefaces for representative works; or select from and write an introduction for the works of one major writer as if for inclusion in an anthology. [Students can even anthologize the works of a creative writing class — their own or those of another class — as my students have for the past several years in an academic summer program for high school students at Oxford University, which brings poets and critics into constructive dialogue with each other.]

3. Engage in tactical iconoclasm. Write a defense of one of Johnson's abused subjects (e.g., *Lycidas* or Collins's poetry). Or write a deliberately provocative critical preface to a poem à la Johnson, imitating his irreverent style; other students can have the option to respond (or submit to a new literary dictator!).

4. Pursue human interest angles. Research and write a brief biographical preface to a favorite (or assigned) author, imitating Johnson's biographical hook technique by using human weakness and foible to narrative advantage. Or compile a collection of humanizing anecdotes about the authors on a class syllabus. Or, in a creative writing class, write a short story or one-act drama based on a scandalous or humiliating secret Johnson reveals in one of his *Prefaces, Biographical and Critical*.

In an age that prizes relevance, these kinds of exercises enable students to apprehend the magnitude of Johnson's historic achievement and at the same time to understand and master the cultural constructs of their own world. In conjunction with readings in Johnson's *Dictionary* and his prefaces (usually under the familiar title *Lives of the Poets*), they help dispel the aura of authority that surrounds Johnson and alienates so many from him. In the end, even as the charlatan Wizard of Oz proved well-meaning, so can Johnson the reputed Literary Dictator emerge as more of a reader-friendly democrat.

On Teaching Johnson and Lockean Empiricism

Timothy Erwin

One of the better ways of sorting out the more significant features of Johnson's work rests in exploring its intellectual contexts. While every serious writer can, and arguably should, be read against an appropriate cultural backdrop, for Johnson the allusive tapestry is surprisingly varied and complex. A chapter in *Rasselas* draws on an early text on aviation, a character sketch in *The Vanity of Human Wishes* is abstracted from a best-selling biography by Voltaire, and the *Life of Savage* occasionally echoes the tub-thumping rhetoric found in the popular magazines of the day. It often seems that Johnson remembered everything he read and found a way of putting most of what he remembered to good use. Much in the same way that the twentieth century has known the influence of Freud, the eighteenth century enjoyed the influence of John Locke. Johnson was born just two decades after the appearance of Locke's *Essay concerning Human Understanding*, and his early career recognizes and comments on the developing influence of Locke on British culture. Quite often in reading Johnson, we understand the intellectual context as a problem addressed, a rhetoric expressed, or a narrative pattern established by Locke's *Essay*. To introduce students to major works like *Rasselas*, *The Vanity of Human Wishes*, or the *Life of Savage* without some consideration of the Lockean heritage would be sadly to miss out on one of the most compelling aspects of reading Johnson: the way he translates the philosophic thought of his age into exemplary scenes of human conduct.

Admittedly, undergraduates may be skeptical when one tells them that the moral philosophy of Locke illuminates the works of Johnson. They should be led to understand philosophy in an epistemological sense — that is, as a guide to the sensibility the writer lived and breathed rather than as an unnecessary complication. Skepticism provides a good point of departure for the classroom discussion of Locke, in fact, because setting limits to what can be known is in large part what empiricism is all about. Empirical philosophy is deeply commonsensical. It was meant to open onto a measured enjoyment of the good life and not onto what Leslie Stephen once called, in characterizing much philosophy before Descartes and Locke, "mere logomachy" (35). Lockean empiricism is as much a way of forming important choices as it is a philosophic system, and its influence is seen in many writers of the period, from Joseph Addison to Laurence Sterne. Let's round off the idea to a common denominator, defining *empiricism* broadly as "the theory that all knowledge is derived from sense-given data, holding that the mind is originally an absolute blank (tabula rasa), on which, as it were, sense-given impressions are mechanically recorded, without any action on the part of the mind."

The definition, which I adapt from the eleventh edition of the *Encyclopaedia Britannica*, serves pretty well as a cultural index even as it blurs an exact understanding of Locke. The definition is useful mainly because it teaches that eighteenth-century Britain generally considered sense perception and especially vision to be a kind of knowledge. As Addison tells us in the *Spectator*, the pleasures of the imagination arise chiefly from the most perfect of senses, that of sight (Tillotson, Fussell, and Waingrow 352). Locke and his compatriots, in other words, agreed for a time that looking carefully at something was the best way of knowing it. That Johnson shared fully in the mental habit explains why he would instruct readers to "cast their Eyes round upon the World" in a periodical essay of his own devoted to finding a middle way between a traditional respect for ancient learning, on the one hand, and modern creativity, on the other (*Rambler* no. 154; Tillotson, Fussell, and Waingrow 100). It was about midway through the four decades during which the writings of Locke enjoyed their greatest purchase on English life, or from about 1725 to 1765, according to Kenneth MacLean (2–3), that Johnson published his verse masterpiece *The Vanity of Human Wishes* (in *Poems* 91, ed. McAdam and Milne). A free imitation of Juvenal's tenth satire, the poem opens with a magisterial couplet —

> Let Observation with extensive View,
> Survey Mankind, from China to Peru

— describing a normative empiricism that Johnson's moral imperative turns in an increasingly active direction. Although the recommendation would later strike Coleridge as redundant, observation does what it must, Donald Greene likes to point out, as an all-inclusive searching into human variety at its furthest poles. The subject of the poem is not geography, of course, but a human nature revealed by different cultures and customs to be essential rather than accidental in its diverse ambitions. The individuals of Johnson's survey, otherwise so unlike, share with the reader a common disillusionment. As readers come to recognize that worldly ambition is entangled in serial disappointment, the poem turns away from "dull Suspence" (line 344) or desuetude toward the sublime peroration of the closing, where the virtues of health, self-control, love, patience, and religious faith are held out as more reasonable human goals. The narrative shift from immediate gain toward the benefits of simple goodness is Lockean as well as Johnsonian. Locke was recognized as an orthodox believer by mid-century, and he endorsed the substitution of greater for lesser moral good as the surest way to divine reward. Despite our normative definition of empiricism as passive, Locke would also have agreed that the final goals named by Johnson could be grasped only by a positive act of the mind; in fact, Locke provides greater warrant for the active moral fervor of the conclusion of the poem than the ancient satirist Johnson imitates. Like the mystic writing pad that served

Freud as model for subconscious memory, the tabula rasa, or blank page, in Locke becomes what C. S. Lewis calls a magistral metaphor (141), a figure useful for recalling a detailed view of the mind but a figure that is also, as an expert on Locke remarks, misleading if taken too literally (Yolton, *Introduction* 82–87, 131–35).

Although the classroom approach I've sketched out here borrows some terms from current criticism, the basic pedagogy is commonplace enough. I often teach the Lockean backdrop as an epistemological *norm*, a term that reader-response criticism uses to name habits of mind already part of the historical sensibility. Teaching and learning are like writing and reading — two halves of a cooperative whole. An instructor wishing to present a complex idea often generalizes by avoiding needless detail, perhaps also drawing a vivid analogy for illustration's sake, and then expects the student to complicate the idea in a carefully considered term paper. In something of the same way, eighteenth-century writers usually reflect complex cultural influences normatively. Several norms enter into a given work at once, of course, either in tandem with or in opposition to one another. None is intellectually or ideologically stable over the long haul. During a semester survey, students might learn that the history of the idea called the *sublime*, for example, not only separates itself from an idea of the beautiful but also discloses a famously unstable notion variously defined as the polemical club Boileau wields against modernism, as half the gendered divide of Edmund Burke, and as the conceptual frame helping to shape the picturesque landscape of Jane Austen and many other eighteenth-century writers and painters.

As we saw, Johnson in *The Vanity of Human Wishes* keeps close to a Lockean norm of observation and patterns the proper fulfillment of human need after Locke. At the same time, the poem deviates from the metaphor of economic interest that Locke uses to describe the laying up of moral goodness and clearly distinguishes gain from virtue, or, in its own terms, gold from good. The stirring of emotion we feel at the poem's close depends, in part, on a conventional intersection of sublimity and religious enthusiasm. All these features may be described according to a norm-and-deviation model. Although there is some risk in posing norms for students — chiefly that of their supposing that once a norm is identified, nothing more need be done with it — they usually recognize that cultural conventions are wholly subject to the rhetoric of the works that incorporate them. In its variety of perspectives, a normative approach offers a reliable guide to historical difference, whether understood as our own distance from past cultures, as their unsuspected heterogeneity, or as the ideological fault lines within them. But like any pedagogical tool, a normative empiricism is useful only to a point and is presented mainly in order to be refined by a firmer grasp of Locke and a better sense of his presence in Johnson. What finally makes the approach valuable for undergraduate teaching is that norms never prove wholly normative. They mediate, instead, between the historical situation and the artful address of the work at hand. Once situated along a broad horizon, the work responds in ways that students can be expected to expand through their own research and close reading, working outward from the elements of language and structure to context and then back again.

Among more particular affinities between Johnson and Locke, three more or less distinct strands of interest invite discussion. The first is linguistic. As James H. Sledd and Gwin J. Kolb write in their pioneering study of Johnson's *Dictionary*, Johnson considered words to be the signs of ideas, to be names arbitrarily imposed by humankind and entirely subject to human custom (26). Locke likewise took the view that while ideas are private and derived singly or in combination from sense impression, the words describing them are sensible, public, and wholly conventional signs. Johnson cites Locke time and again in his definitions. We can look for illustration at the definitions of words important to a major theme in Johnson, the choice of life, definitions I would like to return to momentarily. Locke is cited under the definition of the word *choice* ("Whether he will remove his contemplation from one idea to another, is many times in his *choice*") and also after *will* ("The power, which the mind has to order the consideration of any idea, or forbearing to consider it, or to prefer the motion of any part of the body to its rest, and vice versa") and *motive* ("The *motive* for continuing in the same state is only the present satisfaction in it; the *motive* to change is always some uneasiness"). Recent studies argue convincingly that Johnson's ideas regarding lexical meaning in the *Dictionary* owe a good deal to Locke's theory of language in the third book of the *Essay concerning Human Understanding* (DeMaria, "Theory"; Hedrick; McLaverty). One interesting way of tracing the connection is to list several maxims from Johnson's works on the chalkboard and then ask students to test the keywords against a preference for single or double definitions. Let's take three examples:

> Slow Rises Worth, by Poverty Depress'd
> > (*London*, line 177, *Poems* 56)

> Pow'r has Praise, that Virtue scarce can warm
> > (*The Vanity of Human Wishes*, line 183, *Poems* 100)

> Nothing can please many, and please long, but just representations of general nature.
> > (*Preface to Shakespeare*; Tillotson, Fussell, and Waingrow 1067)

If students are asked to look up the abstract nouns in these sentences, they will find that most of them list several definitions. For some of the nouns, notably *praise*, *virtue*, and *nature*, the different senses enumerated carry with them what lexicography calls an etymon, or kernel of meaning, from definition to definition. In a modern college dictionary their definitions would proceed along a scale of usage from the meaning with the most currency to the meaning with the least. In Johnson's *Dictionary*, by contrast, definitions are listed in a Lockean manner, as moving from a simple to a complex idea. The word *nature*, for instance, begins by naming an imaginary being, as Johnson calls it, or a genius of nature, and then carries that etymological sense through three further definitions. Although well aged, maxims like these will prove a revelation to those who don't yet know them, and at the same time reveal a semantic debt to Locke.

Another affinity concerns the choice of life itself, a theme that is everywhere in Johnson. Often the choice-of-life theme develops in a Lockean direction by setting the orderly selection of rational good against the random gratification of passion. In Johnson the vocabulary of choice is made up of the words *liberty, choice, motive, will, need, desire, passion, suspend,* and *happiness.* For all these and a host of others, Johnson's *Dictionary* cites the chapter titled "Of Power" in the second book of the *Essay* (Alkon 80; C. L. Johnson 565–66). Significantly, nearly the entire discussion of situational willing in Locke is scattered among citations throughout the *Dictionary*. Why should Johnson recur to these pages of Locke's so often if not to locate an important Lockean influence on both contemporary culture and his own narrative? When *The Vanity of Human Wishes* asks readers to consider where they might find proper objects for their hopes and fears (line 343, *Poems* 107), or when *Rasselas* determines that the search for a happy choice of life is finally a choice of eternity, the inquiry reflects the moral psychology of choice in Locke. Conversely, when Locke declares that one should suspend one's desires in order to make a fair examination of the choices that life offers because such consideration is a perfection of human nature (264; 2.21.48), he shapes the moral tenor of Johnson's thought and anticipates a repeated narrative moment in the work. Not surprisingly, Johnson also cites Locke beneath his definition of the verb *to suspend* ("This is the hinge on which turns the liberty of intellectual beings, in their steady prosecution of true felicity, that they can *suspend* this prosecution in particular cases, till they have looked before them"). And yet students shouldn't assume that Locke provides the master key to Johnsonian narrative, anymore than the dream narratives of Arthur Schnitzler, say, belong somehow to Freud. Over the long course of his career, Johnson finds Locke useful in different ways, and his major works articulate select features of the Lockean project.

Joshua Reynolds celebrated what he called Johnson's fondness for discrimination, and the single work that more than any other puts the normative furniture of the second book of the *Essay* on full display is probably Johnson's first major biography, the *Life of Savage*. Let me risk repeating myself by expanding on the relation a bit (Erwin). Richard Savage was a talented if indigent poet whom Johnson met on first coming down to London in 1738. In telling the story of his life six years later, Johnson makes Savage a representative of empiricism, telling us, for instance, that Savage "easily received impressions from objects and very forcibly transmitted them to others" and that he learned from experience to consider the middle state of life the most virtuous (Brady and Wimsatt 581, 603). During the eighteenth century, as Neal Wood points out, Locke was read not so much as disinterested philosopher but rather as spokesperson for a pragmatic, middle-class moral economy (41–64). The most thoroughgoing use of Lockean norms in the biography involves two concepts treated in Locke's discussion of situational willing in the second book of the *Essay*, the concept of due consideration and the distinction Locke draws between a state of liberty and a state of necessity.

Even before beginning to discuss the biography, students are asked to distinguish the different episodes that Savage passes through by looking for certain temporal cues. As the structure of the work unfolds, we decide that what Johnson calls the golden part of Savage's life, the conditional interlude he enjoys with his patron Tyrconnel, is an episode distinct from the others. We also notice that it is somewhat fictional; as the footnotes point out, Johnson's sense of chronology has gone awry. It is fictional in another sense, in that it describes a state of life that none of us is ever likely to experience, not even on the best working holiday imaginable. Then we explore some of the differences between the golden part and surrounding episodes. First of all, the episode is an interval of prosperity that Savage achieves as the result of a bargain struck with his patron. Unhappily, Savage fails to keep his side of the bargain. The golden part affords him a special perspective on social life high and low; with it he is able to receive a variety of impressions, to store them, and to transmit them to others. The privileged interval also allows him to bring out two of his better compositions, his pamphlet satire *An Author to Be Let*, which shows genius as well as a certain lack of consideration, and his long poem *The Wanderer*. In a roundabout way the golden part stresses a central proposition of the biography, that the life of writing is ever subject to situational constraint, or to what Locke calls necessity.

We also notice, on entering and leaving the golden part, that it somehow places Savage "at liberty" and that afterward poor, deluded Savage continues to think himself "at liberty" (Brady and Wimsatt 579, 592) when he is actually not. The term *liberty*, clearly key to an understanding of the episode, also invokes an intellectual context. What might it mean to have one's life be free, to be utterly at liberty? we ask ourselves. What does the enjoyment of personal freedom entail for us today? What might it have meant in the age of Johnson? To worry about these questions in their local philosophic sense, to take the golden part to approximate a Lockean state of liberty, is to read the biography as empirical parable. And there is lexical evidence that Johnson meant us to understand the work that way. *Liberty* is an idea that Locke characterizes as "a Power in any Agent to do or forbear any particular Action . . . preferred to the other" according as the mind shall direct (237; 2.30.8). Johnson follows him in the definition, citing the passage from Locke in the *Dictionary*. We conclude our class discussion by bringing Locke's chapter "Of Power" to bear on a biography that has come to appear more and more like negative moral allegory. After his murder trial, conviction, and pardon, Savage is placed on probation, as it were, where he has the golden opportunity to set before himself the motivational milestones that Lockean liberty requires in showing the way to happiness. Unhappily, he refuses to suspend immediate gratification, reveals a lack of Lockean consideration, and so must contend with the final sufferings that follow.

There are several other implications worth pulling out of the biography, and one of them leads us some way into an ideological intersection of Johnson and Locke. The relation is a qualified one. Johnson points out the lessons of the biography with a vocabulary of calamity and compassion without precedent in Locke, and several themes enter the work only after the influence of the *Essay* has left off. What Charles H. Hinnant elsewhere in this volume aptly terms the rhetoric of biography finally posits a pluralist self for Savage. On the whole, however, Locke's individualist and progressive values are also those of Johnson and the audience he wanted to reach. Of course, Johnson's intellectual independence never allows him simply to repeat Locke's commercial prescriptions for the body politic. In the best empirical tradition, Johnson first anatomizes Locke, tests him, and subjects him to demonstration. Only then, over the course of his long career, does Johnson come to side, by and large, with the sturdy common sense and close consideration of the Lockean way of ideas.

Style and Values: Imitating Samuel Johnson

William Kupersmith

> The greatest and most necessary task still remains, to
> attain a habit of expression, without which
> knowledge is of little use. This is necessary in Latin,
> and more necessary in English, and can only be
> acquired by a daily imitation of the best and
> correctest authours.
>
> —Johnson to Samuel Ford, 1735

In a pioneering and still immensely valuable study of Samuel Johnson's prose style, W. K. Wimsatt, Jr., concluded with a warning couched in a Johnsonian period: "That which is read with admiration in the pages of Johnson, may be discovered with amusement in imitations of his immediate successors, but the further the imitation is protracted by posterity, the greater must be the danger that the effort will excite but a murmur of polite disgust or a smile of frigid indifference" (*Prose Style* 148). It was a fine touch of a witty man to end with a specimen of mock-Johnsonian style. But Wimsatt implies that although writing in the style of Johnson may have had some value for the eighteenth century, it is now essentially a parlor game. That I came to find out otherwise, that students could learn not only from reading Johnson but from trying to write like Johnson, was a happy accident. My own scholarly interests are in classical influences on English poetry, so my Johnsonian knowledge ends with the age of Johnson scarce begun, with the publication of *The Vanity of Human Wishes* (1749). But I regularly teach courses in advanced writing as well as in the literature and culture of eighteenth-century England. Both have provided me with opportunities to introduce Johnson to students, in literature courses as a major eighteenth-century thinker and in writing courses as a master of the classical style of English prose. Approaching Johnson from two such different points of view gives students the opportunity not only to write about Johnson but also to try to write like Johnson and to reflect on the relation between Johnson's values as a man and thinker and his modes of expressing those values.

Because the *Life of Savage* is an early work marked by an abundance of general moral reflections, it is a good starting place in a course in eighteenth-century culture, where it fits nicely into a unit on philosophical or religious thought. The vicissitudes of Savage's unhappy career provide enough variety to hold the interest of students while they accustom themselves to the difficulties of Johnson's prose, and the instructor can bring to their attention passages that illustrate Johnson's style and values well. This one much impressed me when I encountered it as a graduate student in my first eighteenth-century course:

It were doubtless to be wished, that Truth and Reason were universally prevalent; that every thing were esteemed according to its real Value; and that Men would secure themselves from being disappointed in their Endeavours after Happiness, by placing it only in Virtue, which is always to be obtained; but if adventitious and foreign Pleasures must be persued, it would be perhaps of some Benefit, since that Persuit must frequently be fruitless, if the Practice of *Savage* could be taught, that Folly might be an Antidote to Folly, and one Fallacy be obviated by another.   (73–74)

The passage displays a number of features that may trouble a reader new to Johnson. First the diction — "adventitious" is an unusual word whose meaning is not obvious even to the reader who recognizes its relation to *advent*. But it is precisely the right expression here, because it means both "accidental" and "not essentially inherent" (*Dictionary*). Most students will think "prevalent" means "widespread" — a sense unknown to Johnson and that unfortunately appears suited to the context but blurs Johnson's point. To Johnson, "prevalent" means "Victorious; gaining superiority" (*Dictionary*); not that we cannot recognize what is true and reasonable but that we lack the will power to do so. Similarly, the title to chapter 44 of *Rasselas*, "The Dangerous Prevalence of Imagination," is likely to be misunderstood as a statement that too much imagination is dangerous, when what it really means is that we are in danger if our imagination is stronger than our grasp on reality, as happened to the astronomer who thought that he could control the weather.

    In an unmodernized text, the capitals may make the reader wonder whether "Truth and Reason," "Folly," and "Fallacy" should be regarded as personifications or simply as abstractions. Although students should be told that, until the middle of the eighteenth century, printers routinely capitalized all nouns, as in German, reading more Johnson is really the best way to answer the question. *The Vanity of Human Wishes* offers an abundance of examples: "Then say how Hope and Fear, Desire and Hate, / O'er spread with Snares the clouded Maze of Fate" (*Complete English Poems*; lines 5–6); "Fate wings with ev'ry Wish th' afflictive Dart" (line 15); "Where then shall Hope and Fear their objects find?" (line 343). The concepts are not quite personifications, though Johnson can describe them as laying traps and hurling spears. These lines are like the mottoes in an emblem book but without the illustrations. But "Hope and Fear" and the like are not what one critic has called "bloodless abstractions" (Krieger 146). Rather, they represent real psychological forces in the human mind. Similarly, "Fate" is the inexorable nature of the reality without, the objective world that cannot be wished away.

    Johnson's poetry also offers a good chance for students to become acquainted with features of his style that recur often in both his verse and his prose. One might choose for analysis the description of the fall of Cardinal Wolsey in *The Vanity of Human Wishes*:

> At length his Sov'reign frowns — the Train of State
> Mark the keen Glance, and watch the Sign to hate.
> Where-e're he turns he meet a Stranger's Eye,
> His Suppliants scorn him, and his Followers fly;
> At once is lost the Pride of aweful State,
> The golden Canopy, the glitt'ring Plate,
> The regal Palace, the luxurious Board,
> The liv'ried Army, and the menial Lord.
> With Age, with Cares, with Maladies oppress'd,
> He seeks the Refuge of Monastic Rest.
> Grief aids Disease, remember'd Folly stings,
> And his last Sighs reproach the Faith of Kings.
>   (lines 109–20)

The form of the couplet makes the stylistic effects more obvious. If most students in a class have not already studied versification in an introduction-to-literature course, the instructor will have to teach them how to scan; fortunately the regularity of the eighteenth-century heroic couplet makes the principles easy to learn. Instructors might want to consult William Bowman Piper's *The Heroic Couplet*, still the most detailed study of the form, especially the discussion of Johnson's couplet style (396–400). Reading aloud can demonstrate how alliteration, a purely sonic effect, welds the individual couplets into a larger structure. One should notice particularly the repeated sibilants ("Sov'reign," "State," "Sign," "Stranger's," "Suppliants," "stings," "Sighs") and palatals ("Glance," "golden," "glitt'ring," "Grief," "Kings"), as well as the thick cluster of liquids (*l* sounds) throughout the passage and especially in lines 110–16. The combined sonic effects are reinforced by the grammatical structure and versification. Line 114, "The golden Canopy, the glitt'ring Plate," is welded to the preceding line by the rhyme scheme but belongs also with the couplet following because all the items enumerated are in apposition to "Pride" and share the same structure: "the repetition of an identical word or group of words in successive verses or clauses," an effect that classical grammarians called *anaphora*. This rhetorical figure is an emphatic means of creating Johnson's favorite stylistic effect, *parallelism*: the "arrangement of equally important ideas in similar grammatical constructions, often reinforced by verbal echoes" (Beckson and Ganz 12, 191).

In Johnson's prose, of course, the parallels are not so exactly balanced and predictable as this definition would suggest. But if we look back at the passage quoted above from the *Life of Savage*, we see similar patterns: "Value" and "Virtue"; "Pleasures," "Persuit," and "Practice" ("prevalent" echoes both *p* and *v*); "Folly," "Folly," and "Fallacy." Both *Savage* and *Vanity* exemplify a central concern of Johnson's work in the 1740s, presenting "life as a course between temptations" (Lipking 517).

It is Johnson's style of the next decade, though, that has generally been regarded from the eighteenth-century to now as the most Johnsonian. That characterization is appropriate because the 1750s gave us the *Rambler* (1750–52) and the *Dictionary* (1755), Johnson's two most extended and influential works. But, unfortunately, critics have emphasized Johnson's diction. Parodists produced such specimens as this:

> Some *narcotic* seems to have *refrigerated* the red liquor which circu-
> lates in the Doctor's veins, and to have *hebetated* and *obtunded* his
> powers of *excogitation*. . . . Perhaps his admirers may answer, that
> my remark is but the *ramification* of envy, the *intumescence* of ill
> nature, the *exacerbation* of "gloomy malignity."
>   (qtd. in Wimsatt, *Philosophic Words* 67)

Ironically, some of the Latinate words stigmatized are now extremely common, and probably only *hebetate* and *obtund* would give pause to the educated reader today. The parodist also ignored Johnson's syntax, which seldom employs such constructions as a concluding tricolon of three parallel phrases. Johnson preferred contrasting pairs arranged in longer periods, as in the following passage on friendship from *Rambler* no. 64:

> Friendship is seldom lasting but between equals, or where the supe-
> riority on one side is reduced by some equivalent advantage on the
> other. Benefits which cannot be repaid, and obligations which cannot
> be discharged, are not commonly found to increase affection; they
> excite gratitude indeed, and heighten veneration, but commonly take
> away that easy freedom, and familiarity of intercourse, without which,
> though there may be fidelity, and zeal, and admiration, there cannot
> be friendship. Thus imperfect are all earthly blessings; the great effect
> of friendship is beneficence, yet by the first act of uncommon kindness
> it is endangered, like plants that bear their fruit and die. Yet this con-
> sideration ought not to restrain bounty, or repress compassion; for duty
> is to be preferred before convenience, and he that loses part of the
> pleasures of friendship by his generosity, gains in its place the gratula-
> tion of his conscience.   (3: 344)

It seems significant that the difficulty in maintaining a friendship between persons of differing station or fortune should be examined with so many parallels and contrasts: "Benefits" and "obligations," "gratitude" and "veneration," "freedom" and "familiarity," and "fidelity" and "friendship." A cynic might have ended with the comparison between unequal relationships and dying plants; had Johnson done so, we might wish to interject, like Prince Rasselas to Imlac, "Enough! Thou hast convinced me that no human being can ever have a friend." But Johnson was no cynic, and the last sentence reminds us that what is most important is our knowledge that we have acted rightly, even though we may inadvertently arouse resentment and ungratefulness.

One word in the passage may well be unfamiliar to the modern reader: "gratulation." The etymological relation to *gratitude* and *congratulation* is obvious, but its sense is subtly different. It means "[s]alutations made by expressing joy; expression of joy," whereas *congratulation* means the "act of professing joy for the happiness or success of another" (*Dictionary*). That we have lost a friend through our very generosity brings us neither happiness nor success, but it pleases our conscience to know that we have acted rightly. In placing charity above friendship, Johnson shows how far his ethic differs from that of the Bloomsbury group.

At the opposite pole from *congratulation* is found *condolence*: "The expression of grief for the sorrows of another; the civilities and messages of friends upon any loss or misfortune" (*Dictionary*). For most moderns such "civilities and messages" survive vestigially only in the sympathy card; but in Johnson's day, writing letters of consolation was both a solemn duty and an art form. One of the most moving is Johnson's of 1758, written to Bennet Langton on the death in action of Langton's uncle General Dury, which concludes:

> The only reason why we lament a soldier's death is that we think he might have lived longer, yet this cause of grief is common to many other kinds of death which are not so passionately bewailed. The truth is that every death is violent which is the effect of accident, every death which is not gradually brought on by the miseries of age, or when life is extinguished for any other reason than that it is burnt out. He that dies before sixty, of a cold or consumption dies in reality, by a violent death; yet this end is borne with patience, only because the cause of his untimely end is silent and invisible. Let us endeavour to see things as they are, and then enquire whether we ought to complain. Whether to see life as it is will give us much consolation I know not, but the consolation which is drawn from truth, if any there be, is solid and durable, that which may be derived from errour must be like its original fallacious and fugitive.   (*Letters* 1: 111, ed. Chapman)

The relentless logic is striking; imagine now writing a bereaved relation that a death in an air crash was not especially violent. But Johnson wanted to emphasize that Dury's fate was not unlike that of many others and that his family should not feel singled out by misfortune. The construction "Let us endeavour to see things as they are, and then enquire" balances two Latinate verbs that alliterate. Substitute "try" and "ask" and the sense remains the same, but adding more one-syllable words makes the rhythm choppier. Equally balanced are the pairs in the final sentence, which contrasts the comfort offered by "truth," which is "solid and durable," with the "fallacious and fugitive" consolation of "errour." Even under severe emotional stress we must remain realistic and rational.

In teaching Johnson's works to students, I wanted to find out whether they could incorporate Johnson's style in their own writing and, if they could, whether their writing would reflect Johnson's values as well. The following example by Thomas Knight, a junior, was written for a class in literature and culture of eighteenth-century England and was inspired by my remark that Marilyn Monroe might make a superb modern exemplum of the perils of beauty that Johnson describes in *The Vanity of Human Wishes*. Knight instead based his imitation on the *Life of Savage*. Here is an excerpt from "An Account of the Life of Miss Norma Jean Mortenson":

> Several times during the course of her career, despite the approbation of the public, she was ordered from the employ of the film company by the corporation masters. Nearly as many times as her employment was terminated, did she, chastised and full of promises to mend her ways, return to appear before the Cinematograph. It was during a self-imposed hiatus that she made the acquaintance of Arthur Miller, the well-known playwright. He was enamoured of her beauty and she of his intellect, and despite two previous attempts at the ways of love, the couple engaged to be married and carried out their intentions. It is true that it was not a match without some ardour and compatibility, but after four years of struggle with the artistic temperaments of the pair, and coping with the exigencies of public acclamation, Norma Jean and Arthur sought a Bill of Divorcement, and were parted. This was to prove the final impetus toward instability in the life of Norma Jean. Her intemperate use of soporifics degenerated to the dangerous, causing further delays and excess costs during the placement of images on the film of the Cinematograph. Though not without sufficient funds to live a comfortable, if somewhat conservative life, living without the accolades of the public, without assurance of this through her images appearing on the cinematographic film, Norma Jean was inconsolable.

Anachronisms are always a problem in imitation, but by choosing the obsolete form "film of the Cinematograph," Knight both preserves the archaic flavor and uses a word whose Greek roots Johnson would have understood as representing some kind of device that captured movement in images on a "thin pellicule or skin" (*Dictionary*). Johnson's characteristic alliterations are here as well as the Latinisms and parallel constructions, though I doubt that Johnson himself would have paired "of struggle with" and "coping with." But one does not expect the perfect mimicry of the kind of contest set by English weekly magazines Wimsatt, in *Philosophic Words*, deprecated in an undergraduate student's imitation; rather one looks for evidence of an understanding of Johnson's views of life and of his mode of expressing them.

Such evidence is apparent in another example, an imitation of Johnson's epistolary style by Laura Sellner, a senior, who had first read Johnson in my course in eighteenth-century literature and culture a year before, when she thought the *Life of Savage* "served more to entertain than to educate." She continued, in an imaginary letter to Johnson himself:

> When, after nearly the absence of one year, I turned again to your work, not long after the sudden and unexpected death of my brother, whose loss I felt to be one of great potential, I found that your words, more nearly your voice, comforted without bringing pity, and led me to understand what could not be justified. I only regret, Sir, that I cannot more fully express my appreciation for that which you provided. Such eloquent presentations of thought and idea, neither discoloured by passion nor too well-reasoned, become not dogmatic claims for answers, nor unreasonable accounts of life, but represent simply the truest depiction of the human condition that I have yet discovered. If ever you questioned the capacity of your words to endure, I write now to inform you, Sir, that your efforts, however painstaking, were not made in vain, that your impact upon one life has been considerable, that your words are as necessary for future benefit as for present delight.

In reading this paragraph, despite its few jerky parallels, a teacher feels that the student has achieved all that one could hope she would experience in reading and imitating Johnson, to be able to enjoy the pleasures of his text, the beauty of his style, and the rigor and exactitude of his mind. The great satisfaction in teaching Johnson's works comes from sharing his devotion to reason and truth, to seeing things as they are and knowing that whatever small comfort such a cold-eyed and realistic view may give, it will be more lasting than the fallacious and fugitive attractions of error. In enabling students to discover Johnson, we indeed provide a source for future benefit as much as for present delight.

Reading Johnson Psychoanalytically

Gloria Sybil Gross

Like the dream, a creative work offers important clues into the hidden secrets of the mind. If we come to that work with some previous knowledge of the author's life, we are likely to encounter some familiar psychological themes. The life of Samuel Johnson has often been examined from a psychological perspective by literary scholars and psychoanalysts alike, who impress us with the astonishing modernity of the man and his writing. Analytically oriented biographies by James Clifford (*Dictionary Johnson*; *Young Sam Johnson*), George Irwin, John Wain, and W. J. Bate (*Samuel Johnson*), in addition to shorter accounts by W. B. C. Watkins (*Perilous Balance*), Katherine Balderston, Bertrand Bronson ("Johnson Agonistes"), Peter Newton, Roy Porter ("Hunger"), and Bernard Meyer, feature a portrait of conflict and fervent striving so compelling as to make us feel the presence of a living person. Moreover, Johnson himself interpreted psychological themes with an insight remarkable for his time. His ideas are clearly interwoven with his personal development, for he owed a keen understanding of mental phenomena to intense and painful self-analysis. A progressive and enlightened inquirer into human nature, Johnson wrote about the dynamics of personal identity and human relationship, topics of ardent lifelong pursuit. These meanings remain to be tapped by contemporary students struggling with many of the same questions and challenges as he did. A psychoanalytic approach gives us a Johnson who is stunningly a young person's writer, who intuitively grasps and passionately renders enduring patterns of human experience.

I teach Johnson in a number of undergraduate courses, including Introduction to Literature for nonmajors, the Eighteenth-Century Literature survey for majors, and seminars devoted exclusively to Johnson or Johnson and his circle. Typically, the reception is enthusiastic at all levels, differing only by more sophisticated responses, according to the students' breadth of critical and historical background. I attribute this success to the power and range of the psychoanalytic approach, which offers a bracing relevance across culture and ages. Doctrines of psychoanalysis may be persuasively introduced in the classroom as the product of modern intellectual history, with many of its ideas having become part of ordinary educated discourse. Students are therefore intrigued and favorably inclined to interpretations that draw on analytic models. Terms such as *conflict*, the *unconscious*, *inhibition*, *compulsion*, *guilt*, *obsession*, and the like have become common parlance and are readily acknowledged, with the simplest, most concise definitions setting them clearly in focus. Those with advanced exposure to psychoanalytic literary theory may venture on what is au courant — the dynamic relation between reader and text, often linked in spirit to French structuralism and deconstruction. On more traditional grounds, I prefer the approach of classical psychoanalysis, which assumes a coherent relation between Johnson's life, his fantasies, and his creative production. It is a humanistically oriented style of inquiry, which well suits the empirical temper of Johnson's own ideas and attitudes. Needless to say, those who wish to use this method should be acquainted with some basic knowledge of Johnson's turbulent personality and may refer, as they will doubtless direct their students, to the provocative studies by the authors mentioned above.

An informed and attentive analysis of Johnson's life history, indispensable to the vantage point here endorsed, offers students a contemporary search-light playing over the many intricate surfaces of his character. What makes him interesting is not some implausible edifice of his stern literary dictator-ship or moral or religious perfection but the fact of his vulnerable, more truly human responses to the world and its inhabitants. Not least important is the discrediting of antiquated myths of smug autocracy and rigid adher-ence to the status quo, spawned by Boswell's slanted, if ingenious, narrative. By contrast, Johnson's modern biographers emphasize the quality of vehe-ment strife and discord, as well as ambivalent relations to obedience and authority. They call attention to powerful feelings of disapproval and rejec-tion by his parents as a chronic pattern of his emotional life. In effect, John-son's notorious depressive episodes and fears of insanity, both downplayed by Boswell, appear to stem from early childhood fantasies of abandonment and ruin. If these are the constituent factors affecting Johnson's inner world, they are also supported by more tantalizing testimony from his private papers. We are fortunate to have access to those extant, now collected in volume 1, *Diaries, Prayers, and Annals*, of the Yale Edition of the Works of Samuel Johnson. Accordingly, I assign excerpts from the fragment of auto-biography as well as the "Prayers and Meditations" — many students have their interest so piqued as to read the entire selection. My discussion here describes how I use Johnson's private papers to illuminate aspects of the works I normally teach in my senior seminar on Johnson. I concentrate on one work, a rather unduly neglected little allegory, "The Vision of Theodore, the Hermit of Teneriffe" (1748), which Johnson once called the best thing he ever wrote. The essential method may be employed with other texts, as well as in less specialized courses in which Johnson is also taught. A skillful psychoanalytic reading can open fresh and vital ways both to present John-son in the classroom and to understand his extraordinary contribution to the history of psychological thought.

Having assigned outside readings from Johnson's modern biographers, I approach his personal documents as dramatic clues to his deep sense of anguish and tumultuous striving. Under the psychoanalytic lens, his private writings disclose a wealth of meaning behind apparent simplicity. The sur-viving fragment of autobiography entitled "Annals," a kind of stream-of-consciousness narrative, re-creates enigmatic scenes from childhood, ones obscurely remembered or evidently absorbed from descriptions of others. In them, we detect powerful feelings of fear, shame, love, pain, anger, pride, and so on, emerging with all their original strength and clarity. In well-preserved detail we see the exalted picture of his father on horseback as the sheriff of Lichfield, riding the boundaries of the city and feasting its citizens on the day after his birth. And we find the tender image of his mother, visiting her infant son every day at the nurse's house, tending him on the long journey to London and back to "cure" his scrofula by the "Queen's touch," encouraging him in his lessons when he was in danger of failing. " 'We often,' said she, dear mother, 'come off best when we are most afraid.' . . . These little memorials soothe my mind" (14). But for all these benefits, we also note a strained and afflictive atmosphere:

> I was born almost dead, and could not cry for some time. . . . It was discovered that my eyes were bad; and an issue was cut in my left arm. . . . In ten weeks I was taken home, a poor, diseased infant, almost blind. I remember my aunt Nath. Ford told me . . . that she would not have picked such a poor creature up in the street.   (3–5)

Even worse, the dominant impression of Johnson's childhood appears to have been his parents' characterological depression, which could not but lower his own self-image:

> My father and mother had not much happiness from each other. They seldom conversed; for my father could not bear to talk of his affairs; and my mother, being unacquainted with books, cared not to talk of any thing else. Had my mother been more literate, they had been better companions. She might have sometimes introduced her unwelcome topick with more success, if she could have diversified her conversation. Of business she had no distinct conception; and therefore her discourse was composed only of complaint, fear, and suspicion.   (7)

Doubtless Johnson's troubled beginnings left ineradicable traces in his mind, and, as his biographers argue, these experiences in large part directed and influenced the pathogenic course of anxiety and depression suffered as an adult. Our next examination of his devotions calls into even stronger relief the unremitting sense of self-reproach and self-punishment he incorporated from early life. Readers of Johnson's "Prayers and Meditations" — heavily edited as they are by George Strahan, the young clergyman friend to whom he gave them shortly before his death, and a self-appointed guardian of his reputation for religious piety — are invariably struck by the endless recitation of grief, doubt, and self-lacerating guilt. To preserve the integrity of the analytic method, I remind students that we are not concerned here with questions of religious orthodoxy — though, to be sure, Johnson framed many expressions of his mental anguish with religious themes, reflecting a lifetime acquaintance with the Bible, the Book of Common Prayer, and other Christian teachings. It is, however, by way of his professed faith that we approach once more a dominant theme of emotional life, uncommonly open and undisguised. In the resonances of these fitful supplications and piercing laments, we make out his terrifying obsessive fantasies.

The devotions tell over and over of "vain terrours," the "tyranny" of "vain imaginations," "scruples," "perplexities," and "disturbances of the mind very near to madness." Above all, they describe how Johnson created dangerous situations of seduction and assault in the continual round of vows and resolutions he bound himself to and broke. Students need to understand how the syndrome shows him falling in and out of disaster: confessing a wrong, evidently lured to committing it again, and then punishing himself for it. Rife with mounting desperation, Johnson's protests reveal a streak of brinkmanship, to which many can relate, where he is ever the hapless victim. It is astonishing to see how long and laboriously he persevered:

> Easter Eve. 1761: I have led a life so dissipated and useless, and my terrours and perplexities have so much encreased, that I am under great depression and discouragement. . . . I have resolved . . . till I am afraid to resolve again.   (73)

> Sept. 18. 1764. 7 in the Evening: I have now spent fifty five years in resolving, having from the earliest time almost that I can remember been forming schemes of a better life. I have done nothing.   (81)

> Easter Day, Apr. 7. 1765. About 3 in the morning: When I consider how vainly I have hitherto resolved at this annual commemoration of my Savior's death to regulate my life by his laws, I am almost afraid to renew my resolutions. Since the last Easter I have reformed no evil habit, my time has been unprofitably spent, and it seems as a dream that has left nothing behind. My memory grows confused, and I know not how the days pass over me.   (91–92)

> July 22–23: This day I found the book with the resolutions, some of which I had forgotten. . . . Of the time past since those resolutions were made I can give no very laudable account. . . . My memory has been for a long time very much confused. Names, and Persons, and Events, slide away strangely from me. . . . The other day looking over old papers, I perceived a resolution to rise early always occurring. I think I was ashamed or grieved to find how long and how often I had resolved, what except for about one half year I have never done. My Nights are now such as give me no quiet rest.   (157–59)

In the "Prayers and Meditations," Johnson torments and abases himself before an almighty taskmaster, and he begs *"to be loosed from the chain of* [his] *sins*" (81). Originating from the Book of Common Prayer — "Though we be tied and bound with the chain of our sins, yet let the pitifulness of thy great mercy loose us" — the metaphor also refers to an inveterate motif of self-enslavement. In prayer upon prayer, the vicious cycle of broken pledges seduces him to would-be criminality. And heeding this critical issue of emotional life, we are not surprised by the chilling diary entry in Latin: "De pedicis et manicis insana cogitatio" (140), translated "insane thought about foot-fetters and manacles." Neither are we puzzled by Johnson's pleas, in the extraordinary letter he wrote to Hester Thrale in French, to be disciplined by her, nor stunned by the notorious padlock entrusted to her, in view of the deep-rooted impulse to danger (Bate, *Samuel Johnson* 384–89; 438–41; Wain, *Johnson* 286–92; Newton, 101–06). As medical historians have argued, public confinement in Johnson's lifetime was a menacing reality — to wit, his friend the poet Christopher Smart's being institutionalized (Porter, "Hunger" 80). And likely for Johnson, the fantasy of incarceration posed various wishful as well as self-punitive unconscious meanings.

Applying the discoveries drawn from the dark and painful struggle of inner life, we may now view Johnson's writings in the light of his subjective feelings of being persecuted and held in captivity. According to the parable in "The Vision of Theodore," Habit is the inescapable adversary who obstructs the road to the temple of happiness. She often joins with Appetite and Passions, first to entice by offers of assistance, but then to ensnare in perpetual thralldom, those not amenable to proper guidance. Falling into her clutches, mortals are lost to various corruptions: Ambition, Avarice, Intemperance, Indolence, Despair. By contrast, Education, Innocence, Reason, and Religion lead propitiously to the cherished goal. The tale is not unusual for conveying conventional wisdom, except that Johnson appears to have amplified the description of Habit from his principal models (Kolb 115–16). He makes Habit into a fearsome slave driver, and he accentuates how she lures and constrains her victims:

> It was the peculiar artifice of Habit not to suffer her power to be felt at first. Those whom she led, she had the address of appearing only to attend, but was continually doubling her chains upon her companions, which were so slender in themselves, and so silently fastened, that while the attention was engaged by other objects, they were not easily perceived. Each link grew tighter as it had been longer worn, and when by continual additions they became so heavy as to be felt, they were very frequently too strong to be broken. . . . Habit always threw new chains upon her fugitive: nor did any escape her but those who by an effort sudden and violent, burst their shackles at once, and left her at a distance; and even of these many rushing too precipitately forward, and hindered by their terrors from stopping where they were safe, were fatigued with their own vehemence, and resigned themselves

again to that power from whom an escape must be so dearly bought,
and whose tyranny was little felt, except when it was resisted.

(202, 207)

Rampant and dangerous, Habit ever stalks the road to Happiness and turns
it to ruin:

> They wandered on from one double of the labyrinth to another with
> the chains of Habit hanging secretly upon them. . . . They proceeded
> in their dreary march without pleasure in their progress, yet without
> power to return. . . . Discontent lowered in their looks, and Sadness
> hovered round their shades; yet they crawled on reluctant and gloomy,
> till they arrived at the depth of the recess . . . where the dominion
> of Indolence terminates, and the hopeless wanderer is delivered up
> to Melancholy: the chains of Habit are rivetted for ever, and Melan-
> choly, having tortured her prisoner for a time, consigns him at last
> to the cruelty of Despair.   (211–12)

Evidently autobiographical, the portrayal of Habit explains an interior
process of coercion and self-created torture, a potent prototype of Blake's
infamous, grim "mind-forged manacles." Students are impressed by the correspondence between these allegorical denizens and the crippling inhibition
and terror Johnson relates in his private papers. Indeed, the passages may
be read side by side for their sympathetic echoing of each other. Thus we
note how the repeated acts of obsessive behavior and the dreadful paralysis
of will come from a sense of relentless obstruction: in the terms of the allegory, "Habit" blocks the way to purposeful life. In both Johnson's accounts,
her unsparing yoke and enforced drudgery have the quality of compulsions.
With increasing tenacity, Habit gains on her prey, withholding, subduing,
riveting, until the battle waged over consciousness itself appears to be given
up and lost. Human impulse, thus deprived and frustrated, must carry on
its struggle through routes that are constrained and corrupted, where we
anticipate themes of Johnson's future writings: the treacherous paths of
wealth, fame, scholarly ambition, social success, beauty, love, and other
modes of habitual self-delusion.

Doubtless Johnson has much to say to the current crop of twenty-one-
year-olds. If he has renewed himself for each generation of readers, today
is surely a time when we can use him most. Neither the cheerful, shallow
optimism of those who trip giddily toward the next century nor the pallid
lucubrations and massive denial of current academic theorists can claim
much of a stake in the inward life. With such dubious guides, we rarely
approach the essential struggles, the principal motives and feelings behind
human experience — in Johnson's haunting phrase, "that hunger of imagination which preys incessantly upon life" (*Rasselas*, ch. 32). But for Johnson, the

inward life is the galling challenge to complacency and the key to under-standing — and to mastering — a world increasingly ridden by conflict and discontent. No self-satisfied or effete posturing can appease the hunger of imagination. No pat or abstruse solution can quell the irresistible tensions that issue from the deep recesses of the psyche. In the "Habits" of "The Vision of Theodore," the bizarre configurations of *Rasselas*'s happy valley, the vast expanses of wilderness in the Western Islands of Scotland, the recurring metaphors of pursuit, captivity, and escape that pervade his other works — in these more than literary tropes, we find rich sources of psychic meaning. That Johnson wanted them to be found is unmistakable, by virtue of his penetrating and unceasing preoccupation with the hidden order of the mind. Perhaps Johnson himself is the best advocate of all for a psychoanalytic approach, when he states in his famous review of Soame Jenyns's *A Free Inquiry into the Nature and Origin of Evil*: "The only end of writing is to enable the readers better to enjoy life, or better to endure it."

TEACHING JOHNSON TO NONMAJORS

Johnson in the British Literature Survey Course

Raymond-Jean Frontain

Johnson, whose extraordinary intellect and idiosyncrasies of behavior and expression are the subject of the first great modern biography, is paradoxically as much the last great voice of the corporate life as Dante — responsible for the most comprehensive description of the medieval hierarchical universe — is the first writer of the European tradition to express a radical sense of self. For if, as Allen Mandelbaum assures us, Dante's *"io sol uno"* (*Inferno* 2.3) is "the first triple repetition of an 'I' that we have in Western writing" (xiii), Johnson is probably the last great poet to write using the collective voice of abstractions. The period extending roughly from 1300 to 1800 saw the balance gradually reset between the primacy of the public and the private spheres of existence, between concerns for communal welfare and individual happiness, and between the relative importance of inductive and deductive modes of reasoning. This, it seems to me, is the particular urgency for teaching Johnson in a sophomore-level survey course: it is the last chance to allow students to hear a voice, and possibly in its strongest expression, that excoriates pride as vanity (when generally students' only understanding of the term is as used in "to take pride in oneself"), that believes in the possibility of a set of ultimate truths even when painfully conscious of humanity's inadequacy to discover them, and that is not afraid to judge according to a set of right standards even if it must first feel its way through murky uncertainties and dense ambiguities in order to establish them.

Consequently, I have been frustrated that, at all three institutions where I have taught the two-semester British survey course, I have been expected to follow the division established by the editors of *The Norton Anthology of English Literature*, which moves from *Beowulf* to Johnson in the first volume and from Blake to Beckett in the second. For several years it seemed that when I could make it to Johnson at all, it was at the end of an already crowded semester, which allowed me to teach him only cursorily at best. I was particularly frustrated one term to find that — on a comprehensive final essay-examination asking students to contrast attitudes toward the vanity of earthly glory expressed in Hrothgar's advice to Beowulf (Abrams et al., *Norton* 56–57, 5th ed.), Spenser's description of the House of Pride (*Faerie Queene* 1.iv), Milton's Limbo of Vanity (*Paradise Lost* 2.440–97), Swift's Lilliput (*Gulliver's Travels*, part 1), and Johnson's *The Vanity of Human Wishes* — students wrote most hazily about Johnson even though, as the author studied most recently, he presumably should have been freshest in their minds. About two years ago I happily hit on the idea of concluding the first half of the survey course with Pope and Swift, and of reserving Johnson for the beginning of the second, where I might use *Vanity* both as a recapitulation of the Augustan worldview against which the Romantics sometimes felt they were rebelling and as a touchstone against which later expressions of certain recurring values could be weighed.

During my initial class meeting of British Literature 2, then, I review such concepts as the medieval hierarchical view of the universe, the Elizabethan world picture, and the great chain of being, roughly mapping out the idealized dimensions of the premodern world, with its insistence on revelation from above, its respect for authority, its concern with integrating the individual within the social whole, and its reliance on satire as a way of controlling deviant behavior. The advantage of living within such a system, obviously, is that in a created cosmos that inheres with meaning and in which everyone is certain of his or her place, one may rest secure in one's faith in an ultimate source of truth and justice, even when the accomplishment of that justice must be postponed to the afterlife. The disadvantage, in modern terms, is the denial of interiority, of the importance of the individual self and of its powers of observation and deduction. Recalling the inevitable clash we'd seen in earlier literature — between the reality and the symbology of pope and monarch, between truths reached by the individual's light of reason and authoritatively asserted interpretations of divine revelation, and between conclusions inductively arrived at from empirical evidence and principles deductively reasoned through a system of correspondences — I draw on the work of such critics as J. Hillis Miller (ch. 1), Harold Bloom (xiii–xxv), and C. L. Barber (*Creating*; *Whole Journey*) in assessing the role of the Protestant Reformation in creating the modern world. English-speaking Protestantism's emphasis on the need of the individual to read and interpret Scripture according to his or her own inner light, and to follow the commands of the spirit rather than those of the priest, liberated the individual conscience even while traumatizing it with the responsibility for the identification of truth. What is more, even while freeing the individual from the shadow of monolithic belief, the collapse of social systems guaranteeing meaning made inevitable both the modern experience of alienation and the new religion of psychotherapy. Likewise, tolerance of multifarious interpretations and the desire to protect the individual's liberty to practice those beliefs have led inevitably to the secular state in which meaning is democratically reduced to the least common denominator, even while allowing for the stimulation and renewal of free dialogue and ongoing discovery.

Such a shift, I remind students, did not occur overnight, with the Renaissance suddenly dividing human history into two antithetically opposed mindsets as dramatically as Moses parted the Red Sea. Rather, drawing on Yeats's image of two interpenetrating cones, I emphasize how each view is implicated in the other, the Renaissance being but the fulcrum on which the historical continuum balances. To dramatize both the shift in sensibility and the continuity of certain values, I ask students to prepare two poems for our second meeting: Samuel Johnson's *The Vanity of Human Wishes* (1749; *Poems*, ed. McAdam and Milne) and William Wordsworth's "Tintern Abbey" (1798). Both Johnson and Wordsworth are modern authors, just as Shakespeare and Milton undeniably are. But like Shakespeare's tragedies and Milton's *Paradise Lost*, Johnson's poem retains vestiges of the "premodern" mind-set that are entirely lacking in "Tintern Abbey." Thus, although written only fifty years apart, *Vanity* and "Tintern Abbey" operate in radically different ways even while expressing many of the same basic concerns. (I recognize the real danger encountered by using the terms *modern* and *premodern* so loosely, but I have concluded that with nonmajors perhaps the most important thing we can do after helping them develop appreciation and analytical skills is to make them generally aware of the dimensions of Western culture and of how it has evolved.) Students should come prepared for the next class to discuss three sets of questions:

1. Who is speaking to whom, where, and under what circumstances in each poem? And if a dramatic context does not seem to exist for the poem, what is the nature of the voice that is speaking in it?
2. In what ways are the prayers that conclude the poems similar and different? Also, what are the conclusions reached about human existence in the course of each poem that the prayer is predicated on?
3. Finally, *how* does each speaker reach his conclusion? What kind of evidence does he value? What kind of experience has the authority of example for him? What does this tell us about the way he views the world?

When we reunite, I try to lead discussion along the lines described below.

Dramatic Circumstances

Both are prospect poems, but the scenes they survey are radically different. This point is revealed by the stance of the poet-speaker.

Johnson's "prospect" is as abstract ("Mankind") as it is broad ("from China to Peru"). Only an extraordinarily high vantage point — an Olympian one, to be sure — would allow the human eye to encompass the furthest point east on a flat map as well as the furthest point west. In lifting himself high above the world of daily affairs, Johnson's speaker effectively removes himself from the world of flux, enabling himself to judge dispassionately. Wordsworth's "I" likewise surveys a scene, although, as the title of his poem indicates, the distance is not great and the scene has a local habitation and a name: "Lines Composed a Few Miles above Tintern Abbey, on Revisiting the Banks of the Wye during a Tour, July 13, 1798." It is difficult to grow more specific than this. Similarly, if from his Olympian vantage point Johnson's speaker focuses on Augustine's City of Men, Wordsworth's speaker turns his back deliberately on the city in order to free his inner eye; it is not the world of people that most interests him but an inner world.

The relative effects of their respective distances explain something about the voice of each speaker. To survey all humankind demands a high level of organization; the spectrum "from China to Peru" requires analytical gradations. Johnson's closed heroic couplets evidence the control and discipline of his speaker's rational, highly objective effort. Wordsworth's speaker, in contrast, seems almost casually reflective as he gives license to his play of mind. There is a public, at times almost oracular or stentorian, feel to Johnson's poem, as would be inevitable when someone is speaking from such a great height. Wordsworth's ruminative quality, however, is undercut only at the end of "Tintern Abbey" when the reader discovers that the speaker's sister is with him, making his a private meditation that is twice "overheard."

Human Nature versus Created Nature

Both poems reject society's pursuit of the vain and ephemeral and conclude with moving descriptions of the philosophic or untroubled mind that accepts rather than denies pain and suffering as the inevitable lot of humankind. But whereas Wordsworth's calmness of mind stems from a gladness brought about by his relation to beneficent, healing nature, Johnson's resignation is the result of a stoicism assumed after pained meditation on the conditions of human nature. Wordsworth's condition flows naturally from his relation to his environment, whereas Johnson's derives from a determined act of the will implemented only after careful observation and analysis. Wordsworth's joyous spontaneity is likewise in contrast to Johnson's wearied deliberation.

It usually takes some quick classroom maneuvering on my part to distinguish between Wordsworth's "wise passiveness" — that blessed quietude that approaches passivity, even insentience — and Johnson's ideal of the healthy mind. Such nature as reanimates Wordsworth's speaker, healing and restoring his spirit frayed by having lived too long in a city obsessed with getting and spending, has no power for Johnson. W. J. Bate opens his seminal *From Classic to Romantic* with the anecdote of Johnson's impatience with the Thrales' admiration of the scenery when journeying together: "A blade of grass is always a blade of grass, whether in one country or another," he retorted. "Men and women are my subjects of inquiry; let me see how these differ from those we have left behind" (2). For Johnson, happiness "of the only sort to be had in this life, is to be made not found, by an effort of will, by resignation to poverty, toil and death," William Kupersmith (70) points out in his discussion of *The Vanity of Human Wishes*. Thus, while nature may rekindle the flame of joy for Wordsworth, joy for Johnson is often a delusion or, worse, a cause for envy in one's neighbor, frequently with tragic consequences. That life is a state in which much is to be endured and little to be enjoyed seems to be the conclusion of both *Rasselas* and *Vanity*. The differing tones of the prayers with which *Vanity* (resigned) and "Tintern Abbey" (ecstatic) conclude, I point out, depend heavily on the implications of those two radically different understandings of the word *nature*. Whereas created nature lifts Wordsworth above "the still, sad music of humanity," there is no "music" to Johnson's nature, only feverish supplications and agonized groans that it is one's duty to learn to accept.

Models of Authority

I hope for students to grasp that, whereas Johnson attempts to extrapolate from all times and places (from ancient Greece, Rome, and Persia; through Elizabethan, Stuart, and Georgian England; to modern Sweden and Bavaria) a pattern of behavior common to all people, Wordsworth draws from his own experience a model that he, in turn, offers, nominally to his younger and still inexperienced sister, but primarily to his readers. As Morris Golden observes, "in Johnson's [vision], the psychologically whole man continuously shapes chaos, exercising the will and imagination — on the advice of the observing reason — into valid generalizations upon which to act; in Wordsworth's, the imagining self, the figure creating ties to all that it senses and conceives, becomes the high archetype of the species" (101). This shift in epistemology not only is reflected in the poets' differing choices of verse forms and poetic diction but opens classroom discussion on an important question: the relation of "imitation" to "originality."

Concerned with "How rarely Reason guides the stubborn choice, / Rules the bold hand, or prompts the suppliant voice" (*Vanity*, lines 11–12), Johnson employs the heroic couplet, which is both a visual and an aural display of balance and control. The poem presents itself as a rational exercise: only after Observation surveys, remarks, and watches does it express the conclusions it has formulated. The heroic couplet formally reflects the Johnsonian view expressed in the poem — that humans must exercise restraint and not give in to passionate impulse. Wordsworth's free verse, in contrast, flows as smoothly as the waters of the Wye, the speaker's thoughts rising from some deep inner reserve of memory as the waters roll from their mountain springs. The poem's seeming lack of structure mirrors the mystical process by which the speaker is laid asleep in body and becomes a living soul (lines 45–46). Thus, if Johnson's heroic couplets aim at the completion and finality that come after careful observation and reflection, Wordsworth's free-flowing verse enacts the collapse both of his identity within nature's and of Dorothy's experience within his (she is now as he used to be).

Wordsworth's well-known comments about the artificiality of neoclassical poetic diction bear summarizing at this point in our discussion as well. As Golden notes, Johnson's is an "evaluating self abstracting general laws from human experience" (107). Poetic abstractions, thus, have deep meaning for him, being all that is finally visible in the realm of human affairs when Observation surveys humankind from the Olympian vantage point that holds China as well as Peru within its view, and being all that can be "said" after Observation has surveyed, remarked, and watched. Wordsworth's poetic self, however, is acutely *self*-analytical. In a sense, the speaker in "Tintern Abbey" is what he sees (I = eye), his inner self awakened by the experience that nature allows him. Tintern Abbey is not in itself a symbolic or emblematic location, like Pope's Windsor Forest or Gray's Eton College; any set of ruins might have served Wordsworth's purpose as far as ruins go. Rather, the place is significant because of the speaker's three visits there; his experience confers as much importance on the place as the spirit of nature has conferred on him. Wordsworth's language is, thus, as I-centered as Johnson's is abstract. It is not that Johnson does not see individualities or particularities but that he does not want the reader to be distracted by differences he feels are on the surface only (the stripes of a tulip). An eminently sociable poet, Johnson is more interested in what people share; he learns by closely observing and abstracting from society, not by distancing himself from the social realm to discover his deeper self in nature. His poetic abstractions bear eloquent witness to that sociability.

Finally, comparison of the two poems provides a perspective for examining questions about poetic originality and authority. By giving *Vanity* the subtitle *In Imitation of the Tenth Satire of Juvenal*, Johnson emphasizes the parallels between Augustan Rome and Georgian London; his survey is of what is constant in human nature, not of what is peculiar to any one time or place. Students who have read Gray's "Ode on a Distant Prospect of Eton College" with me in the earlier half of the course, however, may object that Wordsworth's "Tintern Abbey" is not entirely an "original" production and may have a similar generic indebtedness. Instead of getting lost in a debate over our understanding — or misunderstanding — of the relative merits of imitation and originality, I ask students to consider why Johnson felt that it was important to acknowledge a poetic source or model while Wordsworth thought it better to emphasize his independence, both socially and poetically.

A close study of *The Vanity of Human Wishes* provides students with several important concepts:

1. The exercise firmly establishes Johnson as the last great voice of neo-classicism in students' minds. Of all the writers studied in the survey semesters, Johnson is perhaps thematically closest to Milton. Although the passage is not present among the *Norton* excerpts, *Vanity*'s prayer echoes Michael's reproof of Adam's revulsion before a vision of mortality:

> Nor love thy Life, nor hate; but what thou liv'st
> Live well, how long or short permit to Heav'n.
> (*Paradise Lost* 11.553–54)

Similarly, it echoes *Samson Agonistes*'s concluding praise of "calm of mind, all passion spent" (Abrams et al., *Norton* 1634, line 1758, 5th ed.). Advocating the acceptance of what is divinely ordained *because* it has been divinely ordained, Johnson's *Vanity* gives evidence to an orthodox religious mind-set for which there is increasingly less voice in the modern world. Thus, in terms of the broad movements of Western culture, Johnson is far closer to Dante than to Wordsworth in this regard. The same can be said of his attempt to control passion through poetry: Dante's terza rima is as regular as Johnson's heroic couplets, the discipline that the poet imposes metrically on his material mirroring the moral discipline that the individual must impose on personal experience. The verse of Dante and Johnson teaches the reader self-discipline, whereas the free verse of Wordsworth, meandering as the mind does in a moment of calm, deliberately pursues an existence apart from the social whole, thus valuing the individual and personal experience above the social order.

2. What the examination of *Vanity* traces, in fact, is the historical process of the foregrounding of the individual. A radically different sense of self is expressed in Johnson's and in Wordsworth's poems, and Johnson's is certainly the more alien of the two to contemporary students. Today's commercials bombard students with encouragements to "be all that you can be" and not to skimp when faced with the choice of a more expensive hair coloring agent "because you're worth it." Likewise, successful political campaigns are based on the appeal to greed: "Are you better off than you were

four years ago?" Johnson's excoriation of pride as vanity, his Christian-stoical acceptance of inevitable disappointment, and his heroic endeavor to over-come any challenge offered to his mental composure suggest values that have not been entirely lost to the modern world but have lost the better part of their currency. One hopes that their purchasing power can be restored, even if only for the week's time we spend in this study.

3. Finally, at the same time, our exercise illustrates W. J. Bate's warning against periodization (*From Classic to Romantic*). Despite its powerful neo-classical ethos, Johnson's poem is modern in its expression of a worldview that is, on a limited level, not far from that of T. S. Eliot's *Waste Land*. And despite the strong Christian faiths of each poet, neither poem displays a facile moral optimism, a conviction of "grace abounding." Johnson may conclude his poem with a prayer, but there is no infusion of salvific grace from another world, as in Spenser, no deus ex machina, as in Greek drama. Johnson's is essentially a secular world in which human beings are on their own to legislate their behavior and can only trust to reason to do so cor-rectly; they must suffer through their mistakes. The model of *Vanity*, of course, is the Book of Ecclesiastes, which, unlike its fellow piece of Wisdom literature, the Book of Job, is not informed by a voice from the whirlwind asserting divine control of human affairs. By living in a world in which the miraculous is notably absent, Johnson has more in common with Eliot than with Dante.

I remain happy with this exercise. It offers a way of recapitulating the premodernist worldview as we begin talking about Romantic self-conscious-ness, at the same time offering Johnson as the semester's first great intro-duction to the particularly modern experience of doubt regarding the value of human action. *The Vanity of Human Wishes* is a particularly strong transition text, allowing me to refer back to Milton and Spenser as easily as forward to Arnold and Eliot. Reading him at the beginning of the second half of the survey makes Johnson something of a touchstone by which we evaluate all that follows in the term. *Vanity* anticipates Shelley's "Ozy-mandias" and other Romantic poems on transience, although it clearly lacks what Thomas McFarland calls the Romantic love of "ruins." Likewise, attention is called to Romantic reliance on the visionary and the subjective by their very absence in Johnson. Given to suggesting paper topics along the way, I propose three after this exercise: a comparison-contrast of the poet in chapter 10 of *Rasselas* with Wordsworth's Preface to *Lyrical Ballads*; a Life of Wordsworth as written by Johnson (in a Steve Allenesque "meeting of minds"); and, as an indication of how much *Vanity* defines the ethos of the recognizably modernist world, a comparison with the depiction of disappointed hopes, unsatisfying interpersonal relations, and petty vanities — not to mention the controlled anguish of the poet-speaker — in Eliot's *Waste Land*.

Johnson in a Western Civilization Course

Ann Engar

At the University of Utah, I teach in the Freshman Seminar program. Over the three-quarters of their first year, the students learn about Western culture in a chronological sequence. Spring quarter is the "modern" period, beginning with Galileo and Descartes and ending with Woolf and Sartre. During this quarter I have three to four weeks to discuss the important writings and intellectual currents of the eighteenth century: how the writers were influenced by past ideas, how they were influential in their own times, and how they continue to affect us today. Students are encouraged to examine their own values and beliefs as these conceptions are challenged or supported by the texts. *Rasselas* is an important component of my discussion of eighteenth-century thought, specifically in its attacks on utopias, its exploration of the sources of happiness, and its assumptions about the human mind.

I begin the eighteenth-century section of the course by lecturing briefly on Newton and the *Principia*. Students read selections from Pope's *Essay on Man* to see an example of cosmic optimism, the importance of reason, and the continuance of chain-of-being ideas. Then we spend three days on *Candide* discussing Voltaire's satire on "Whatever is, is right," on the unreason present in the world, and on the desirability of utopias.

After *Candide* I devote three or four days to *Rasselas*. I start with a brief biography of Johnson (spending at most ten minutes). I contrast his life with Voltaire's: his middle-class background, his limited formal education, his struggle to survive in London, his work on the *Dictionary*, his life as a professional writer, and his later life in which his ideas inspired and challenged Edmund Burke, James Boswell, Joshua Reynolds, and others. Students see in him the emerging figure of the professional writer and the eighteenth-century quest for organized knowledge (the philosophes and the *Encyclopédie*, Voltaire and his *Philosophical Dictionary*).

For the first day we focus on issues in the happy valley section of *Rasselas*: Johnson's attack on utopias and chain-of-being ideas and his exploration of the human mind and its requirements for happiness. When discussing El Dorado in *Candide*, I have already reminded the students of the myths of a golden age or paradise lost that we have covered over the course of the year: Genesis and Arthurian legend as well as the ideal worlds of Plato's *Republic* and More's *Utopia*. I tell students that the dream of an ideal state will resurface in the writings of Marx and Engels and in the worlds of modern science fiction. Now, while reading *Rasselas*, we contrast the greed, the need to be better than others, and the romantic reasons for Candide's leaving home with Rasselas's reasons for leaving the happy valley. I ask students whether they themselves would like to live in El Dorado or the happy valley and why or why not. Then students explore why both authors, publishing within months of each other, picked the subject of happiness and the inability of human beings to remain content.

On the second day, to prepare the class for our discussion of Rasselas and Nekayah's journey in search of a "choice of life," I ask students what they believe are requisites to happiness today, and we list the responses on the chalkboard: knowledge, success, goals, health, and self-confidence are frequently given. Students are encouraged to redefine those requisites on the basis of the questions Johnson raises. Is activity necessary to happiness? What are the roles of the imagination, desire, and hope in happiness? Does knowledge really lead to happiness? How does comparison of ourselves with others enhance or diminish happiness? Should or can happiness, by definition, be something "solid and permanent, without fear and without certainty" (*History of Rasselas* 45, Oxford ed.)? Must it be accessible to all? How necessary is money to happiness? Can one be happy without the companionship of other people? How necessary is change in our lives? Can happiness be found? The class then reviews the other significant statements about happiness that we have read over our year of study, especially those by Aristotle and those in Ecclesiastes. I mention Aristotle's statements on the importance of external goods or wealth, freedom, psychological goods (including friendship, creativity, and self-esteem), and virtue from his *Ethics*, books 1, 7, 9, and 10. Then we recall the assertions of the preacher in Ecclesiastes on the importance of having good food to eat, good work to do, and a good wife and of fearing God. I note, too, that critics as early as Boswell have compared *Rasselas* with Ecclesiastes.

If there are four days for discussion of *Rasselas*, we spend the third day in small groups. The object of this day's work is to keep students from pigeonholing *Rasselas* as a work only about happiness and to help students see in a limited way the many issues Johnson raises. Each group receives one of the following sets of questions to explore:

1. What does Johnson's opinion of women seem to be? Characterize Nekayah and compare and contrast her with Cunegonde. What does Nekayah find out about the lot of women? Why does Rasselas take his sister along on his discovery of life instead of a lover? What difference does this choice make in the story and in our feelings in reading about the women in the tale?

2. What does Johnson say about youth and age? What are the merits and difficulties of each stage of life? Do you agree with the ideas presented? As you may remember, Cicero in *De Senectute* said that old age, especially accompanied by honors, has influence worth all the pleasure of youth put together. Would Johnson agree?

3. *Rasselas* belongs to a long tradition of writings on princes and their education. What does Rasselas discover about power and its administration? How important are observation and the study of

history in his education? What kind of persons, military or scholarly, pragmatic or virtuous, make the best rulers? How do the ideas on rulers and their education presented in *Rasselas* compare or contrast with Plato's on his guardians and philosopher-kings and Machiavelli's on the prince? [Students have recently reviewed these ideas, as we have covered Hobbes and Locke.]

4.   The eighteenth century is a time of immense reverence for science and belief in progress based on scientific achievement. How does Johnson seem to feel about science? Is it good or bad for human-kind? Does scientific development have any connection with moral development?

5.   During the eighteenth century, writers questioned their need for a god and the existence of God. We have discussed Voltaire's and Hume's criticisms of Christianity. What does Johnson seem to think about God, faith, and the afterlife? Look carefully at chapters 31, 34, and 45 of *Rasselas*. Compare and contrast Johnson's ideas with those we have read this quarter in Pascal's *Pensées* and Descartes's *Discourse on Method*.

6.   We have seen writers wrestle with the problem of human suffering from the very beginning of our studies in the Hebrew Bible, particularly the Book of Job, through stoic philosophy and the New Testament to Pope's *Essay on Man*. What does Johnson seem to say about suffering? How much trust does he put in reason to handle the complexities of human existence?

I give students thirty minutes to discuss the questions and choose a representative to report their findings to the rest of the class. These questions get students to read and examine the text, to focus their thinking, and then to use the texts to expand into the larger issues and themes we have been exploring throughout the year. Also, depending on the ideas I emphasize in the particular year I am teaching, I may choose one of these areas to highlight rather than happiness and utopias. I recognize that I demand much of my students in answering these questions, especially in remembering other works we have read. But I find that, by continually having to think and talk about past writers we have read, students retain their ideas and better understand their importance.

While the students are working on their questions, I move from group to group to listen to their ideas and give them guidance. In group 1, I remind students of the salon movement about which they learned when reading Voltaire. I tell them that Johnson had close friendships with women, including Fanny Burney. They contrast Johnson's interest in issues of women, marriage, and family with Voltaire's emphasis on romance (and its speciousness). Students look closely at chapters 25 and 39 of *Rasselas*, where women are portrayed as wasting their talents in private life and in harems. They contrast these women with Nekayah and Pekuah, who seem more like the intelligent and lively women of the salons.

I warn students, however, that Johnson still assesses women according to their value to men. Pekuah condemns the harem women for hopping like birds from room to room and frisking like lambs living a life of pure sensation, yet she herself judges their worth only with reference to their value to the chieftain: their beauty is casually dismissed, their talk tedious, and their affection worthless. Pekuah, in contrast, is valued because of what she can contribute to a man: the chieftain seeks her out for conversation, teaches her about the stars, and even leaves her to govern in his absence. Likewise, Nekayah is displeased by the "childish levity and prattle" of the women in private life because she has been able to associate with men such as Imlac and Rasselas. (For further discussion of *Rasselas* and women, see Hansen's helpful essay.) *Rasselas* can thus be used to show that although female intellect and society are increasingly appreciated in the eighteenth century, women are still largely valued by their worth to men and develop only through association with men.

In group 2, I encourage students to look at the beginning of chapter 4, Rasselas's words to the young men in chapter 17, the princess's reflections on parents and children in chapter 26, and the discourse with the old man in chapter 45. These passages can be used to counterbalance the enthusiastic wish fulfillment of Cicero, but I also find them useful as I begin to discuss Romanticism and the Romantic praise of the innocent wisdom of youth in Wordsworth's "Tintern Abbey."

In group 3, I suggest that students look closely at chapter 27, "Disquisition upon Greatness," and Imlac's discourse in chapter 30 on the importance of a study of history in a prince's education. Though Johnson is known as a profound moralist and Machiavelli is sometimes judged to be a moral monster, their analyses of the problems of power based on problems within the human spirit and condition are not so different. The two agree that any ruler must depend on underlings to inform and minister, underlings who will — purposefully or not — mislead, betray, and become jealous of other ministers. Rasselas's inability, at the end of the tale, to fix the numbers of his people and the boundaries of his state certainly reveals Johnson's understanding of the allure of power. Moreover, Imlac admits that, because humans are swayed by their affections, no one can always discover and reward merit or always be just. But Imlac's views also challenge Machiavelli's: because of human nature, Imlac asserts, princes cannot always act to benefit the state or themselves. These views undercut, as well, Plato's concept of the philosopher-king who always acts to benefit the state and personifies wisdom and justice. I try to get students to recognize that, through Imlac's statements, Johnson seems to assert that a just state in which the majority of inhabitants are happy is impossible.

Insofar as education is concerned, *Rasselas* leaves the rarified air of the happy valley: he would not be content with the noble yet censored education given to Plato's philosopher-king. Nor would he be satisfied with the prince's military exercises and study of history as solely a study of power. Imlac values history for its enlargement of the prince's understanding and emphasizes that a prince must be well-rounded: "If accounts of battles and invasions are peculiarly the business of princes, the useful or elegant arts are not to be neglected; those who have kingdoms to govern, have understandings to cultivate" (74). *Rasselas* thus fits well into the class's continuing exploration of the individual and the state.

In group 4, the students focus on the episode of the aviator and Rasselas's conversation with Imlac about the technological achievements of European society versus the backwardness of his own people. In the conversation, Johnson recognizes the achievements of the Western world, yet the aviator episode complicates this vision. I ask the group whether Johnson has faith in progress based on science, a faith they will see demonstrated as they read Condorcet. I also ask students to think about whether Johnson is implying, through the aviator episode, that human beings will not be able to fly, that they are guilty of the pride of Icarus and Daedalus in reaching too far. I mention, too, that Johnson himself performed chemical experiments in a special oven in the Thrales' kitchen garden (Bate, *Samuel Johnson* 435).

In group 5, I comment that Christian beliefs have had remarkable flexibility and longevity throughout the tumults of the twentieth century. Johnson's statements in *Rasselas* serve as useful correctives for students who assume that, after Voltaire's "Ecrasez l'infâme" and Hume's "Of Miracles," all eighteenth-century intellectuals abandoned faith. Students look carefully at passages in chapters 31, 34, and 45 to find rational and psychological arguments for belief: the universality of belief in spirits, the need to believe in absolute moral laws and eventual justice (the moral argument), the hope for a state in which happiness can be found and virtue attained — arguments that Imlac reinforces when he speaks of the lives of the Saint Anthony monks (the argument from desire). I also suggest that students think of Plato's world of the forms and of Cartesian dualism when they read the episode of the visit to the catacombs, particularly Imlac's statement that "all the conclusions of reason enforce the immateriality of mind, and all the notions of sense and investigations of science concur to prove the unconsciousness of matter" (119).

In group 6, the students analyze the lecturer's speech in chapter 18 and identify its Platonic and stoic elements: the need for the higher faculties of reason to predominate over the lower faculties of passion and imagination, the comparison of reason to the uniform and eternal light of the sun, the immunity from fear and grief. Then students debate the sufficiency of Platonic and stoic reason to deal with the sufferings of human existence, basing their discussion on the lecturer's inability to handle his grief over his daughter's death. I stress Johnson's recognition of the personal and emotional as fundamentally human and not necessarily inferior to reason.

Some years when I teach this course there are not enough students to fill six groups, and some classes are better at analysis than others. I have presented what I do with the largest and brightest of classes; some adaptation and scaling down may be necessary.

On the final day of discussion of *Rasselas*, I build on the previous day's work to explore the issues of marriage and family, reason, and the need for society in the episode of the astronomer and in the conclusion in which nothing is concluded. At this point it is helpful to list the characters of the tale on the board and identify the issues with which each is concerned: Imlac with education and poetry; Nekayah with family, friendship, and pastoral life; Rasselas with politics; Pekuah with female education and monastic life; and the astronomer with the dangers of the imagination.

To discuss marriage and family life, we focus on Nekayah and Rasselas's debates on single versus married life and children, in chapters 26, 28, and 29. I use the following questions to spark student interests: Does family life lead to happiness for human beings? Would life with the family as the state (as in Plato's *Republic*) be preferable? Is marriage the "dictate of nature"? The students' investigation of Nekayah's and Rasselas's views serves them well as we encounter the marriage question in Dickens's *Hard Times*; it also helps meet the goal of the class to see the relevance of Johnson's writings to students' own lives.

I use the episode of the astronomer for various purposes. His problem effectively illustrates Hume's contention that human beings see only the sequences of nature and not its causes, a contention that the class learned about when we studied Locke's *Essay concerning Human Understanding*. The astronomer's predicament also illustrates Kant's dilemma of believing in something that reason cannot demonstrate and the senses cannot verify. I mention the astronomer later when, in *Reflections on the Revolution in France*, Edmund Burke says how small a stock of reason each individual possesses and how necessary the use of collective minds is. I further use the episode of the astronomer to show that, in Johnson's view, friendship and society are vital.

My students enjoy discussing how and why "nothing is concluded" at the end of the tale. Having worked through Johnson's view of the mind, the imagination, the importance and dangers of desire and hope, they feel satisfied although the ending leads to no firm resolution. Here I like to draw students' attention to the metaphor of the Nile throughout *Rasselas* and the "flux of life."

The next day we move into a study of Romanticism and spend three days on Jean-Jacques Rousseau. *Rasselas* provides an important counterbalance for this study. When we talk about the Romantic hero, I remind students that Rasselas in the happy valley is a caricature of a Romantic hero, looking for inspiration from his environment, feeling trapped by his society, wandering solitaire, bemoaning the days of his childhood "while nature was yet fresh and every moment shewed [him] what [he] had never observed before" (8), and dreaming idealistic dreams of rescuing orphan virgins. We review the setting of the happy valley, with its terrible and sublime chasms. I also show Kenneth Clark's *Civilisation* film *The Worship of Nature*, which centers on Rousseau but also includes Johnson's criticism of Romanticism (Clark, *Personal View* 275).

When students finish their exploration of Rousseau, I give them an essay examination on eighteenth-century thought. Questions I have used focus on the views of society and its effect on the individual in Voltaire, Johnson, and Rousseau, and the satire on cosmic optimism in *Candide* and *Rasselas*. For a longer and more involved term paper, I ask students to trace one of the large themes we have explored over the course of the year, and students include *Rasselas* when they write about the search for happiness, the development of psychology, utopias and distopias, the individual and the state, humans and their environment, images of women in literature, or marriage and the family.

Although I try to use the ideas I have given here when I present *Rasselas*, I am sometimes overcome by the problems of teaching a wide-ranging introductory course: there is not enough time, or students become enthusiastic about one of the various topics discussed to the exclusion of others (and the latter is not always a bad thing). I do emphasize, however, that Johnson — with his Christian beliefs, views on the nature of men and women, critique of reason, and exploration of the operations of the mind — contributes uniquely to the Western tradition.

TEACHING SPECIFIC WORKS

Samuel Johnson's View of America:
A Moral Judgment, Based on Conscience,
Not Compromise

Brenda Ameter

"I am willing to love all mankind, *except an American*," I announce as I walk into the classroom on the first day my students are discussing Johnson. Having caught the students' attention, I tell them Johnson suddenly burst forth with these words one April evening in 1778 when he and Boswell were sitting with a group of friends discussing the meaning of friendship in the Quaker faith. Johnson then "breathed out threatenings and slaughter," referring to the Americans as "Rascals — Robbers — Pirates" and crying out that he would "burn and destroy them" (qtd. in Boswell, *Life* 3: 290, ed. Hill and Powell). I ask the class why Johnson was antagonistic toward America in 1778. They, of course, always respond that America was at war with England.

American students know surprisingly little about English history except as it relates to the American Revolution, but they have been drilled in American colonial history. My approach to Johnson is to explore his view of the American colonies, building on the knowledge the students already possess. I use a portfolio of material containing selected essays showing Johnson's beliefs that England should not have established a colony in America, that the people living in the colonies should not mistreat the native people, and that the American planters should not set up an economic system based on slavery. The topics make Johnson's opinions vital and interesting to students concerned with important issues in today's society. The class analyzes Johnson's antagonism before the American Revolution and then traces his response to the war.

Before discussing Johnson's views, I carefully point out that a significant segment of influential British society supported the American desire for independence, just as many Americans preferred to remain loyal to England. I stress that British and American attitudes toward the war varied greatly from person to person. Even people with similar positions on the war often differed in their reasons for their views. I encourage students to develop critical thinking skills throughout this unit and to avoid making generalizations about either country. I also note that in historical reenactments of the Revolutionary War, the narrators avoid labels depicting members of either army as "traitors" or "patriots."

Many students in a general education English literature course have never heard of Samuel Johnson; those who are familiar with him often say he was a reactionary who opposed change. The most attention-capturing stories, such as the one used to introduce this unit, may make him seem to oppose liberty and freedom. However, an analysis of Johnson's attitude toward the colonies before the Revolution shows that it was his concern for the rights of all people that brought about his dislike of the English colonies in America. To understand his attitude toward America, one has to place his comments and his writings in the context of his deepest beliefs concerning the relation of an individual to humanity and to his or her country.

Without giving the students prior knowledge of Johnson's view of colonization, I assign material and ask them to write a brief analysis of their responses to the sections of the essays discussing colonization. Students present their interpretation of the material to the class. In a discussion following the individual presentations, students not only compare and contrast their interpretations of Johnson's views but examine their own responses to situations in which the United States faces political dilemmas concerning intervention in other countries. The purpose of the unit has been accomplished when students cite Johnson to support their own views.

"The State of Affairs in Lilliput," the first of a series of articles published in June 1738 in *Gentleman's Magazine*, introduces the class to Johnson's views. Johnson always presents some language and syntax problems for students in a general education class; however, most of the students follow the main thrust of his argument that Lilliput (England) has not gained much from its colonization of Columbia (America) because a country only benefits from such acquisitions when colonies are small enough to be protected against intruders and near enough to the parent country that supplies can be easily provided ("Debates"). Before reading Johnson's discussion of the financial burden placed on England by its colonial policy, most students believe that England benefited financially from its colonization of America. They also think that England committed an injustice in its taxation of America, yet few had ever considered the expense incurred by Britain while exploring, developing, and protecting its new colony. Considering the Revolution from the British point of view provides immediate interest, and students often say they would like to read a discussion of the war in a history book written for students in British schools.

The class then turns to Johnson's political pamphlets to learn more about his objections to the colonization of America. In "An Introduction to the Political State of Great Britain" (1756) the students read Johnson's analysis of Britain's unfriendly relations with its neighbors. While he lists three reasons — the establishment of the Protestant religion, the extension of trade, and the settlement of the English colonies — for the dissension, much of the essay focuses on the third reason, the colonization of America. The students learn that England's expectation of discovering great quantities of gold and silver led it to seize the land in America without considering the obligations incurred by such actions (*Political Writings* 130). They also analyze Johnson's discussion of the origins of the Dutch-English war, and they note that as he is writing the essay, the British are preparing to fight the French. Many students agree with Johnson's exposure of the myth that a country's power always increases as its possessions are extended. Students who are familiar with the Vietnam conflict often find a correlation between the attempts of France and the United States to colonize Vietnam and Samuel Johnson's view that expansion is frequently achieved at great cost. The first time I taught this course I was surprised by how much students know about the Vietnam conflict and how quick they are to relate this knowledge to Johnson's essays.

The next two essays provide an opportunity for the students to view Johnson's objective analysis of the war between France and England. In "Observations on the Present State of Affairs" (1756), Johnson points out that there is no way to judge whether France or England is wrong in the dispute (*Political Writings* 186). In *Idler* no. 20, Johnson gives the history of the war first from the English standpoint, then from the French, emphasizing that it would be impossible to determine which country was in the wrong (*Idler* 62–65). Again students find this material interesting because it gives a different view of the war from the one they learned in American history class. Their responses to this essay nearly always mention Johnson's discussion of historical accuracy. Beginning with his assertion that "no crime" is worse than the "violation of truth" (62), students apply this statement to the differing views of wars with which they are familiar. They then examine his idea that people believe whatever gives them the most pleasure rather than what is true. When Johnson relates this lack of concern for truth to differing countries' accounts of historical events, the class empathizes with his view, for the students have been exploring this point throughout the unit.

As a concluding activity to the material on colonization, the class writes a short essay defending or attacking one country's colonization of another. The students may choose England's colonization of America or any other nation's colonization with which they are familiar. As an alternative activity, they may compare and contrast the view of England's colonization set forth

by Johnson with the view they held before reading the essays. After they
have submitted the essays, the students work in groups examining the compositions to determine whether bias exists.

In the next activity, after analyzing the material on colonization, the students return to the essays to discover Johnson's attitude toward Native Americans. Before they read the essays, I ask them to write what they expect Johnson's attitude to be. They scan the essays until they come to sections dealing
with this topic and compare their expectations with Johnson's statements.
In the "Lilliput" essay, Johnson describes the treatment that he feels the
English have given the Native Americans:

> The People of *Dequlia*, or the *Lilliputian Europe* . . . have made Con-
> quests, and settled Colonies in very distant Regions, the Inhabitants
> of which they look upon as barbarous, Tho' in simplicity of Manners,
> Probity and Temperance superior to themselves; and seem to think
> that they have a Right to treat them as Passion, Interest, or Caprice
> shall direct, without much regard to the Rules of Justice or Humanity.
> ("Debates" 285)

The writing presents some difficulty for many students; however, scanning
the essays several times in search of material on assigned topics increases
the students' familiarity with both Johnson's diction and his syntax. Having
mastered the material on colonialization, they feel a sense of accomplishment when they can easily understand those passages while searching for
ones relating to Native Americans. Students express surprise and pleasure
when they study Johnson's views toward Indians. Although I teach in a location in which few Native Americans reside, this topic is one about which
many students have intense feelings. Most students express these feelings
in their initial written response to the material, and each student has the
opportunity to explain his or her views to the class. Students who talked
little during the unit on colonialization usually respond much more freely
during this section.

While "Lilliput" shows Johnson's dislike of the colonists' treatment of
Native Americans, students receive a more detailed discussion of the issue
in "Political State of Great Britain," in which Johnson contrasts the French
treatment of the Indians with that of the Spanish. Students generally list
the following points in their responses to the essay: the French first abused
the Indians; however, they quickly changed their behavior, and through
intermarriage and cohabitation, enlisted the Indians' support for France;
the Spanish killed thousands of Indians and, because they never attempted
to reconcile them to Spain, lost the empire for the Spanish king (*Political
Writings* 136). During class discussion, I ask the students to consider the
passage in which Johnson points out that the French have the advantage
over the English because of their friendship with the Indians; however, he

emphasizes that they have earned this advantage because of their "virtue" (150). This term, "virtue," provides an interesting topic for class discussion. I mention Bakhtin's point that every word has a different meaning depending on the speaker and the circumstances in which it is used. I then ask what "virtue" means here, how its usage differs from the meaning commonly ascribed to it, and what significance the word has when applied by an Englishman — Johnson — to the French. The students usually respond enthusiastically to this discussion.

Since the students have just read an essay in which Johnson praises the French for treating Native Americans in a humane manner, they often say they are surprised when they consider the material about Native Americans in "Present State of Affairs," because Johnson devotes much of the essay to the crimes committed against the Indians by the British and the French. Students list the offenses and then add any others they are aware of that took place in eighteenth-century America and compare and contrast them with the mistreatment of Native Americans today. The majority of the students feel as outraged as Johnson did about the treatment of Native Americans. Johnson's anger becomes apparent when he says of the war between France and England, "Such is the contest that no honest man can heartily wish success to either party" (186). Usually a few students point out that Johnson felt strongly enough about his topic to make a statement bordering on treason; other class members feel that such comments should not be made when one's country is at war. Occasionally a student knows enough about dissent in the 1960s in the United States to draw parallels between the two forms of disagreement with government policy. This material results in provocative class discussions. Students agree with Johnson that the Indians did not give their land to the foreigners; most find his statement — "The American dispute between the French and us is therefore only the quarrel of two robbers for the spoils of a passenger" (188) — a powerful expression of their own views regarding the seizure of land from Native Americans.

Johnson's expansion of this point in *Idler* no. 81 builds class interest. In an essay that is easy for the students to read and respond to, he dramatizes the condition of Native Americans by portraying a chief telling of the golden past when his ancestors ruled society and nature. This idyllic life came to an abrupt end when strangers invaded their territory, killing a multitude of his people and enslaving others. Two points particularly move the students. The first comes when the chief asks what reward could induce a person to give up land to another: "Fraud or terror must operate in such contracts; either they promised protection which they never have afforded, or instruction which they never imparted" (253). The second, mentioned in nearly every student's response to the essay, appears when the chief says that the strangers could not teach their religion, for they have violated one of its first precepts, that of the golden rule.

This material introduces a class discussion centering on Johnson's depiction of Native Americans. I ask the students to give examples of the portrayal of Native Americans in other works. Usually they include James Fenimore Cooper's Indians, as well as works about famous Native Americans such as Cochise and Geronimo. The class then reads *Rambler* no. 172, in which Johnson dramatizes the value all people place on novelty by telling of an Indian in Virginia who was so delighted with a lock on his door that he spent all day turning the key. Johnson concludes the story by saying, "I doubt whether this paper will have a single reader that may not apply the story to himself" (148). The students compare and contrast Johnson's characterization of Native Americans with the portrayal by other writers and conclude that he draws sensitive human beings. By this time, the members of the class greatly admire Johnson; they understand that part of his dislike of America stems from his disapproval of Britain's colonization policy as well as the colonists' barbaric treatment of the native peoples. Most of all, they relish his insistence that Native Americans have the same aspects of humanity, the desires and wishes central to existence, that people of all races, times, and countries share.

As they begin the unit on slavery, the students feel a sense of camaraderie with each other and with Johnson. They trust him to continue to respect the dignity of others. Johnson does not fail them. Much of his dislike of America came from his hatred of slavery. To help the students place Johnson's thought in context, I give the following facts before they analyze his views of slavery. During his lifetime, Johnson saw the phenomenal growth of slavery in America as the number of slaves carried in British ships rose from five thousand in 1697 to fifty thousand in 1770 (Coupland 22). Boswell expresses the most commonly accepted British view of slavery when he objects to those who have tried to have Parliament outlaw slavery, which he feels necessary to commerce and sanctioned by God (*Life* 3: 203–04).

The students briefly return to "Lilliput," "Political State of Great Britain," and *Idler* no. 81 for short comments by Johnson on slavery. However, his most powerful and cogent attack comes when he helps Boswell defend a slave who sued for freedom after being brought to Scotland (Boswell, *Life* 3: 202–03). The students again prepare informal responses to the selection and share them with the class. The following points come forth during this discussion: Although slavery has existed in many countries throughout the ages, it cannot be considered people's natural state, since all humans began as equals and slavery came into being only through the subjection of one race to another; people may lose their freedom through crime or war, but their loss cannot be entailed upon their descendants. After the students discuss these points, I tell the class of Johnson's relationship with the Jamaican man Francis Barber, whom Johnson raised, educated, and named his heir. The class then notes that Johnson fought slavery in his writings, conversations, and private life.

Before introducing the final essay, I bring in material that shows that Johnson's statement at the beginning of the unit was an exaggeration. He was proud when an American edition of *Rasselas* was published in 1772. Also he wrote a gracious letter to an American in which he says, "You are not mistaken in supposing that I set a high value on my American friends" (*Letters* 1: 305–06, ed. Chapman). The final work for this unit, "Taxation No Tyranny," sets forth Johnson's beliefs that the Americans had no right to rise against England. The students analyze the essay in groups and then present Johnson's arguments and their own rebuttals to the class. During their presentations, most of the groups express admiration for Johnson's comments on slavery at the end of the essay.

As the class concludes its discussion of Johnson's view of America, I bring in Charles McCamic's work *Doctor Samuel Johnson and the American Colonies* and tell students that, according to McCamic, Johnson wrote "Taxation No Tyranny" because he received a state pension (22). As indignation floods their faces, I ask the question with which I began the unit: Why was Johnson antagonistic toward America in 1778? This time the answers center on England's colonization of America and the treatment of the Native Americans and African Americans by the colonists. The students realize that Johnson was greatly angered by the war, but his antipathy to America started long before the Revolution. The Samuel Johnson my students come to know well is a humanitarian, whose thinking and writing on human dignity express ideas three hundred years in advance of his time. As the class moves into a study of his poetry and dictionary, they carry with them the image of a man who writes powerfully on what are possibly the most important subjects of both his age and ours.

Hearing Epistolick Voices:
Teaching Johnson's Letters

Bruce Redford

The subject of "the great epistolick art" (Johnson to Hester Thrale, 27 Oct. 1777, *Letters*, ed. Redford) directs us immediately into a dusty wing attached to the central block of Johnsonian studies. Perhaps "lean-to" rather than "wing" would be more accurate, since scholarly discussion of Johnson's letters has tended to prop itself modestly on the independent structures of biography and criticism. Pedagogy takes its cue from scholarship, circumventing the letters or saluting them at a distance. It is now time to make bold claims for this significant part of the Johnsonian canon, to move the letters decisively center stage. But how does one shake off the dust and take possession?

At least two difficulties need to be overcome. The first of these is the lack of accessible texts: Frank Brady and W. K. Wimsatt, for example, include only eleven letters in their anthology, and Donald Greene sixteen (including excerpts) in his (*Samuel Johnson*, Oxford ed.). The second difficulty is both aesthetic and methodological. Where do the letters fit into Johnson's oeuvre and the great tradition of eighteenth-century letter writing? How should one present and evaluate them — as biographical sources? as cultural vignettes akin to the conversations in Boswell's *Life*? as commentaries on such projects as the *Dictionary* and the *Lives of the Poets*? or even, à la Balderston, as pathological documents?

I have no easy answers to these and related questions — only a conviction that Johnson's letters richly merit, and abundantly repay, the kind of close scrutiny we automatically accord the "major" works. Such scrutiny, it should be emphasized, is informed by contextual understanding without depending on it. When teaching *London*, for example, we make reference to contemporary politics but avoid reducing Johnson's "mournful narrative" to the status of commentary on the contemporary scene (Bloom and Bloom). So, too, we must honor the artistry of an epistolary text instead of treating it as a curio or an archival fragment.

Basic questions of theory and procedure are best formulated in terms of Johnson's own criteria for a genre — a *literary* genre — that he both distrusted and cultivated. These criteria can be deduced from four indispensable commentaries on letter writing: *Rambler* no. 152, two letters to Hester Thrale (27 Oct. 1777, 11 Apr. 1780), and a penetrating critique from the Life of Pope (*Lives* 3: 206–08, ed. Hill). On "epistolary intercourse," as on other literary topics, Johnson was far from being a systematic critic. In one place he condemns its inherent "fallacy and sophistication"; in another he appears to exalt a medium that captures "every thing . . . as it is thought" (3: 207; to Hester Thrale, 27 Oct. 1777). Underlying all his shifting pronouncements, however, is the rejection of extravagant claims for the familiar letter: that it constitutes "a Window in the bosom," allows for stylistic "undress," or promotes unmediated communication (Pope, *Correspondence* 1: 155, 2: 23). Johnson's ad hoc commentaries also suggest that letter writers should banish "ceremony" and "vanity" in favor of "that interchange of thoughts which is practised in free and easy conversation" (*Rambler* 4: 108). The ideal is a letter both "copious" and "distinct," one that captures a speaking tone of voice in the service of "that social officiousness by which we are habitually endeared to one another" (to Hester Thrale, 20 July 1775, 20 Nov. 1783).

The next step is to connect theory with practice: the issues that Johnson engages, with ironic indirection as well as explicit commentary, can be illustrated most effectively by a close look at several letters of consolation. Letters of this kind not only focus key questions of self-presentation, stylistic decorum, and implied readership; they also continue Johnson's lifelong project as Christian moralist, while adapting it to the private, microcosmic form of the familiar letter. It should not be difficult, therefore, to place the letters securely in a context created by analyses of the *Rambler* or *Rasselas*. If time permits, one ought to consider five letters: to Hester Thrale, 17 March 1773; to Hester Thrale, 25 March 1776; to Mary Cholmondeley, 6 May 1777; to Thomas Lawrence, 20 January 1780; to Hester Thrale, 5 April 1781. Three are of utmost importance—those of 25 March 1776, 6 May 1777, and 20 January 1780.

One might start out by asking what a letter of consolation should include, what difficulties it entails, and why in the twentieth century it seems to have fallen into eclipse. The basic challenge, it could be suggested, is to devise a way to communicate and to stylize emotion in the face of a mystery that strains or even obviates language: to steer between the extremes of empty formality, on the one hand, and undisciplined lamentation, on the other. With this thought in mind, one could then turn to the most immediately accessible of the letters (to Hester Thrale, 25 Mar. 1776).

This letter follows a four-part structure that Johnson devised as early as 1760 (writing to James Elphinston on the death of his mother). The first part consists of a declaration of fellow feeling, based on an experience that Johnson shares or anticipates sharing. The sufferer and the consoler are thereby placed in direct personal communion. Johnson then takes a steady look at the hard facts of human mortality. His simplest, bleakest formulation of these facts occurs in the letter of consolation to Mary Cholmondeley: "We all live on this condition that the ties of every endearment must at last be broken" (6 May 1777). Such a refusal to evade, suppress, or take refuge in platitudes reflects Johnson's belief that one must "endeavor to see things as they are" (to Bennet Langton, 21 Sept. 1758). From "things as they are" he then moves to things as they will be—or, at the very least, to things as they can be hoped for, according to the Christian dispensation. Finally, he often concludes with an injunction to activity, to reimmersion in "the business of life."

The letter to Hester Thrale adapts this structure to an occasion of extreme anguish: the death at an early age of an only (and highly promising) son and heir. Two monosyllabic sentences (at the beginning of paragraphs 2 and 3) compose a simple, lyric epitaph, which at once expresses and distills Johnson's own pain: "Poor dear sweet little Boy. . . . He is gone, and we are going." After each of these two sentences the act of distancing begins, in part through stylistic elaboration, in part through doctrinal allusion: monosyllables give way to polysyllables, simple to compound and complex structures, the raw fact of death to the promise of afterlife. Both paragraphs, in short, exemplify the strategy of the letter as a whole: to bear witness to individual grief, to create a community of two (consoling writer and grieving receiver), and finally to invoke a larger society of believers.

In the second half of the letter, which opens with an echo of the Book of Common Prayer, Johnson's voice changes from that of fellow sufferer to that of guide and even priest. A position of relative equality gives way to a ceremonial order based on the hierarchy of preacher and congregation. Injunctions and imperatives enhance the liturgical aura: "Remember first that your child is happy, and then, that he is safe not only from the ills of this world, but from those more formidable dangers which extend their mischief to eternity." Johnson actually played the role of secular celebrant in the solemn yet intimate drama of his final parting with Catherine Chambers (*Diaries* 116–17); his account of that scene offers a telling analogue to this section of the letter. In the concluding sentence, by contrast, hierarchy dissolves as Johnson's voice resumes its tones of uncomplicated affection: "I am, Dearest, dearest Madam, your most affectionate, humble Servant."

This letter (like all those mentioned above) both prescribes and enacts a movement from passion to tranquillity, from raw grief to poised acceptance. It is shaped along formulaic lines, but with a delicacy, wisdom, and compassion that turn homiletic commonplaces into healing art. The letter helps to explain Johnson's preeminence in the genre of consolation, illustrating as it does a style that combines authority and ease. The combination of these two qualities communicates a poise that has been wrested from suffering and consolidated by faith.

Johnson's letters of consolation illustrate both the consistency of his central preoccupations and the versatility with which he adapted those preoccupations to a form that might have seemed ill suited to his gifts. An encounter with the letters, in fact, will overturn (or at least complicate) the stereotypes students may harbor — that Johnson is consistently solemn in tone, dogmatic in purpose, and monochromatic in style. Moreover, the theme of versatility, of Johnson's multiple voices, can provide an effective point of departure for close textual analysis. Without straining for parallels, one might suggest that Johnson offers us epistolary versions of the multiple public genres in which he worked. Thus in scanning his oeuvre, one finds the letter as prose satire (to Lord Chesterfield, 7 Feb. 1755), the letter as comic exemplum (to Hester Thrale, 20 July 1771), the letter as elegiac meditation (to Giuseppe Baretti, 20 July 1762), the letter as secular homily (to James Boswell, 8 Dec. 1763), the letter as travel narrative (to Hester Thrale, Sept. 1773), and the letter as practical criticism (to David Garrick, 12 Dec. 1771).

This spectrum of subjects and approaches is worth documenting for its own sake. To achieve pedagogic order in variety, however, I urge that discussion be concentrated on Johnson's deployment of allusion. As a learned writer at the end of the Renaissance tradition, Johnson could (and did) exploit a vast cultural repertoire of texts, events, images, assumptions, and strategies. As teachers we are accustomed, indeed compelled, to acknowledge this repertoire as it informs a text such as the "Levet" elegy. But the letters draw even more extensively and subtly on a shared inheritance; therefore, most of them cannot be understood without at least limited access to it. Fortunately, brief glossing offers immediate and substantial rewards.

Through allusion, specifically literary allusion, Johnson achieves what Christopher Ricks teaches us to observe in Dryden and Pope: he "creates meanings, comprehends judgments, and animates experiences, by bringing into play other works of literature and their very words" (209). All three activities can be observed in two markedly dissimilar letters, the celebrated repudiation of Lord Chesterfield and the equally famous farewell to Hester Thrale. I would like now to consider these letters in some detail, as a means of suggesting certain procedures that can be extended to much of the surviving corpus.

Johnson begins each of the three central paragraphs of the Chesterfield letter with a literary reference. Only one of these does he signal explicitly: "The Shepherd in Virgil grew at last acquainted with Love, and found him a Native of the Rocks." This haunting gesture toward eclogue 8, in which Damon laments the cruelty of "saevus Amor," anticipates the corrective redefinition that forms the climax of the letter: "Is not a Patron, My Lord, one who looks with unconcern on a Man struggling for Life in the water and when he has reached ground encumbers him with help." But the two earlier allusions have gone far toward preparing for this sardonic repudiation.

In the first sentence of the second paragraph ("When upon some slight encouragement I first visited your Lordship"), Johnson adapts part of the opening line of Georges de Scudéry's epic poem *Alaric* as that line was filtered through Boileau's *Art Poétique*. What he performs, in short, is a complicated act of double allusion, which challenges the reader to recognize both sources, as well as their relevance to the immediate context of the letter. Why this particular strategy? First, it characterizes Chesterfield as he saw himself, a supremely cultivated aristocrat with a high Gallic polish. Second, it introduces the first note of irony — irony that is directed, for the time being, at the writer and not the recipient. The epic line removed from context immediately acquires a mock-epic resonance, which is intensified by the medium of transmission, Boileau's *ars poetica*. Boileau quotes the line ("Je chante le Vainqueur des Vainqueurs de la terre") as an example of the way *not* to begin a poem, sketching the figure of a maladroit, ranting author, woefully deficient in poetic savoir faire. Boileau juxtaposes this blunderer to what he calls "cet Auteur plein d'adresse," a Chesterfield-like figure who speaks with a "ton aisé, doux, simple, harmonieux" (Boileau 175). Such a gentlemanly poet, unlike the uncouth blunderer, eases his readers adroitly into the poem instead of assaulting them with ferocious pseudosublimity.

What Boileau offers Johnson is a contrast that can be made to echo and reinforce the contrast between the gauche lexicographer and the polished patron. For all its subtlety, however, the allusion remains essentially extrinsic to the thrust of the letter, which moves from faintly self-mocking irony to icy sarcasm. The knife begins to twist in the next two sentences: "When I had once addressed your Lordship in Publick, I had exhausted all the Art of pleasing which a retired and uncourtly Scholar can possess. I had done all that I could, and no Man is well pleased to have his all neglected, be it ever so little." The figure of the slightly ridiculous would-be "Vainqueur" turns into that of the cloistered "Scholar," who will abjure the "Art of pleasing" if it licenses such neglect as Johnson has suffered.

The reprimand sharpens in the next paragraph, which contains a buried allusion to the second book of Horace's satires: "Seven years, My lord, have now past since I waited in your outward Rooms or was repulsed from your Door. . . ." The seven years Johnson waited in vain differ all too markedly from the seven years Horace describes in his satire, years of discerning patronage from the generous Maecenas. Maintaining all the while a tone of glacial courtesy, Johnson tellingly insinuates the contrast between true and false patronage, seven years of plenty in the past, seven years of famine in the present. The force of the paragraph does not depend on recognition of the Horatian paradigm, yet the classical frame of reference gives special pungency to Johnson's critique.

From epistolary satire we move next to elegiac lamentation and two letters that draw their power from an emotional topography reminiscent of Vergil's underworld (*Aeneid*, bk. 6). Both letters illustrate Johnson's mastery of what might be called "organic" (as opposed to "decorative") allusion — allusion that functions as the principal bearer of meaning. In the earlier of the two letters, Johnson places a reference to crossing the Styx (Vergil's *irremeabilis unda*, 6.425) at the center of a lament that defines his own sense of exile in terms of classical prototypes (Redford, *Converse* 233–35). Johnson maps out, and then mourns over, a temporarily unbridgeable gulf: he is in Lichfield ("the field of the dead," according to his *Dictionary*), Hester Thrale in Streatham ("home," the land of the living).

In Johnson's final letter to Hester Thrale, the same Vergilian reference occurs, this time embedded in a parabolic reference to Mary, Queen of Scots. As Mary Lascelles ingeniously demonstrates, Johnson "sought to express wretchedness and foreboding" by retelling an inaccurate version of the queen's departure for England ("Johnson's Last Allusion" 37). Johnson knew what had happened in actual fact: the queen crossed the Solway Firth by fishing boat. Yet he turns to a fictionalized source for the analogy it offered to the situation at hand:

> When Queen Mary took the resolution of sheltering herself in England, the Archbishop of St. Andrew's attempting to dissuade her, attended on her journey and when they came to the irremeable Stream that separated the two kingdoms, walked by her side into the water, in the middle of which he seized her bridle, and with earnestness proportioned to her danger and his own affection, pressed her to return. The Queen went forward. — If the parallel reaches thus far; may it go no further. The tears stand in my eyes. (8 July 1784)

The analogy (or "parallel") is clear: queen is to archbishop as Thrale is to Johnson. However, a telling shift of emphasis occurs. In Johnson's probable source the queen is the focus of attention, the archbishop a supporting player; in the letter, the archbishop earns at least as much sympathy as the queen. To enforce his version of the story and the "parallel," Johnson associates the river dividing the two kingdoms with the English Channel, which Hester Thrale may soon be crossing if she makes the terrible mistake of settling in Italy. The mythological dimensions of this river, however, are ultimately of more importance: as "irremeable Stream" it suggests the river of death that will soon divide them forever. The conflation of Vergilian epic with Scots historical mythology turns the letter into a poignant gesture of lamentation, warning, and farewell — all the more poignant for the absence of the savage aggression that characterizes its predecessor (to Hester Thrale, 2 July 1784).

"As letters are written on all subjects, in all states of mind," Johnson observes in *Rambler* no. 152, "they cannot be properly reduced to settled rules, or described by any single characteristic; and we may safely disentangle our minds from critical embarrassments, by determining that a letter has no peculiarity but its form, and that nothing is to be refused admission which would be proper in any other method of treating the same object" (*Rambler* 5: 45). One of the rewards to be gained from teaching Johnson's letters is the opportunity to illustrate their range ("all subjects, all states of mind") while stressing their "peculiarity," their formal reshaping of familiar themes. To adopt Johnson's own terminology (5: 47), we can observe that his epistolary collection includes both "diamonds" and "pebbles." Disentangling our minds from critical embarrassments, we must now set out to show how the diamonds have been cut and the pebbles polished.

Teaching the *Dictionary*

Allen Reddick

Does it really make sense to attempt to teach Johnson's *Dictionary of the English Language* to undergraduates or to speak of this giant monument as we would any other text in Johnson's oeuvre? We can certainly teach the work as a milestone in English lexicography, discussing as best we can its place in the study and development of English; we can also — as most of us teaching a course on Samuel Johnson have probably done — approach the years during which Johnson compiled the *Dictionary* (1746–55) as marking a crucial period in his life. But the appeal to students of such historical and biographical assessments (superficial as they necessarily are) is limited, even when sweetened with the requisite personal references to the "funny" entries, like *oats, lexicographer*, and *excise*. Is the *Dictionary* analyzable like other more obviously "literary" texts? Does it even make sense to speak of Johnson as the author of such a work? Theoretical and critical movements of the last twenty years, particularly semiotics and deconstruction, have taught (or reminded) us that any text can be read critically and that the distance between traditionally literary texts and nontraditionally literary texts is often illusory. But, we and our students may object, isn't the *Dictionary* (Johnson's, like most others) really the product of a mechanical operation, a necessarily generic product of an age, interesting perhaps for this reason, as a historical artifact, but lacking the individualized voice (Johnson's funny entries and personal remarks under a few entries notwithstanding) we generally associate with literary works? In this essay I would like to suggest ways of deepening our students' understanding of the significance of the *Dictionary* to the history of lexicography and language use, and to Johnson's thinking and beliefs, and, in the process, to consider the rhetorical aspects of the work, the dynamic between reader (or user) and text, and the voices and tensions active in the *Dictionary* throughout. I have found that we can help the student identify the crucial relation in the work between intention and fact, between the author's desire and the text's own life and power. This relation is important for an understanding of the work, as well as of the life and writing of Johnson.

Why have a dictionary? What is its purpose? Whose is it? What gives it authority? Who enforces its authority? How do you compile one? Where do you get your words? Do they — the words or the dictionary — ever go out of date? What renders them antiquated? How much should a dictionary say about a word and its use? Should a dictionary record language as it is used, or teach how it *should* be used? And how do we determine whose language is to be the standard?

These thorny questions, and other related ones, are invariably provocative in a classroom setting (involving, obviously, such important issues as truth, propriety, class, power, race, gender). They prove particularly fruitful in discussions of Johnson's great *Dictionary*. I have found that the creation of the *Dictionary* is an effective way into the work, both in my teaching and in my own criticism and scholarship. Questions of origin and methodology are crucial to understanding the aims of dictionaries, as a brief examination of the remarkable history of the *Oxford English Dictionary*, for instance, makes clear. To begin with, both students and teachers should consider the historical and cultural context of the *Dictionary* and its conception and construction (see Reddick; Sledd and Kolb; Clifford, *Dictionary Johnson*).

The need for a large dictionary of the English language formed from consensus (that is, by a nationally recognized body or group), marking an attempt to record proper usage and to control what were considered the excesses and degeneration of the language, had been perceived since the end of the seventeenth century. The Italian Accademia della Crusca had produced its great *Vocabolario* as early as 1623 and the Académie Française the *Dictionnaire* in 1694. The English were far behind in their own lexicographical efforts, and major writers, including Dryden, Defoe, Swift, and Pope, and various prominent political figures, worried publicly about the English neglect of the language (it is useful, if time permits, to have students read relevant selections from these writers on the state of the English language). Although dictionaries of English certainly existed, including Nathan Bailey's series beginning with his *Universal Etymological English Dictionary* in 1721, none commanded the wide influence or cachet of the French or Italian, for they demonstrated no evidence of being formed from a basis of consensus, nor did they contain the kind of prefatory material or other commentary that would place the work into a serious philological, linguistic, social, and historical context. Sensing the void in the market, a consortium of five leading London booksellers in 1746 combined to request from Johnson — a man of sound but limited reputation as a poet, critic, translator, and journalistic writer — a description or scheme of an English dictionary. Johnson's scheme was comprehensive and impressive, convincing the group to sign a contract with him on 18 June 1746, in which they agreed to finance the composition and publication of the dictionary.

The *Plan of a Dictionary*, announcing Johnson's intentions to the public (and dedicating his work to Lord Chesterfield, in the absence of a linguistic or literary academy, as the public representative of concern for the English language), was published in 1747. By this time Johnson had hired several amanuenses (eventually there would be six) to assist him in the selecting and copying of illustrations from English writers as authorities for his words and definitions and to help him with other tasks as well. The inclusion of literary quotations would be Johnson's most obvious lexicographic advancement, and it would require the most effort. He boasted that the work would take him three years to complete; in fact, he encountered serious problems with the incorporation of illustrations, the establishment of definitions, and the variety of language use in written sources, forcing him to abandon both method and manuscript in 1749 or 1750, and recycle his material into a new form. Soon after this failure, the booksellers, frustrated with the virtual absence of completed copy, challenged him to produce his work, but Johnson threatened to strike, and they were forced into silenced acquiescence and continued financial support. In 1752, after a long decline, Johnson's wife died, sending him into a debilitating state for months afterward, during which time he did no work of any kind. Eventually, pages of copy were prepared and printed; in early 1755, with the last sheets being printed, Johnson was forced to rebuff the public attempts of his supposed patron, Lord Chesterfield, who had apparently neglected the project, to gain from his association with it. In his celebrated letter to Chesterfield of February 1755, Johnson responds to his ill-informed and condescending praise of the work, rejecting the imprimatur of the great man's patronage. Having been awarded an honorary degree from Oxford in the same month, Johnson could instead assign to himself the authority of a great university (in lieu of an academy) on the title page of his *Dictionary*, which appeared in April 1755. The *Dictionary* was appropriately formatted in two large folio volumes to encompass, in the view of many, the monument to British nationalism and to literary and linguistic superiority.

As an explanation of his attempts, and apology for the results, the preface to the *Dictionary* is the obvious place for students to identify Johnson's intentions regarding language and this work in particular. Furthermore, the preface is a discrete part of the work, frequently anthologized (one source is Greene, *Samuel Johnson*, Oxford ed.), and easy to discuss. One can therefore treat it separately and, in the process, read Johnson's remarks against or into the body of the *Dictionary* to highlight the more dynamic and interesting parts of the text of the word list. Some of the questions we may ask our students are as follows: Is Johnson consistent in his positions and statements on language? How does Johnson feel about linguistic authority? What does he think that a dictionary can (and cannot) do?

I encourage students to read the preface carefully, to discover for themselves that Johnson assumes the ironic figure of the man with boundless aspirations and expectations, in his enthusiastic adoption of the position of orderer of English language and letters, only to meet inevitable failure and deflation in the execution of an impossible task. One can point out (or help the students to discover) that Johnson's prose and rhetorical structure are highly effective here in part because the subject provides him with an actual example, from his own experience, of the formula of expectation-disappointment or delusion-reality that characterizes his moral writing, rather than a hypothetical, composite, or generic example found in the *Rambler*, *Idler*, or *Adventurer* essays, or in *Rasselas*, or elsewhere. The students should notice that in explaining the methods and procedures he followed in composing the *Dictionary*, Johnson consistently uses tropes or expressions of struggle, defeat, or impossibility, of compromise or surrender, which a reader can find in most paragraphs.

Two of the most famous and distinctive examples form two lengthy paragraphs in the preface (pars. 57 and 72). They follow the same self-mocking, ironic pattern and retain a similar tone, adopting a position of sobering disappointment and deflation: in the first paragraph, in the search for literary illustrations ("When I first collected these authorities. . . . Such is design, while it is yet at a distance from execution . . ."), and in the second, in the search for words and meanings and in the entire design ("When first I engaged in this work. . . . But these were the dreams of a poet doomed at last to wake a lexicographer"). The ironic shape of these paragraphs, which can be compared with a part of a character sketch from the *Idler* or the *Rambler*, reflects the actual outline and spirit of the process of conceiving and creating the *Dictionary*. Johnson describes his own experience and expands it into a paradigm of human nature and hope. These paragraphs, and indeed the preface as a whole, are examples of Johnson's finest moral prose.

The way to illustrate Johnson's dilemma as a lexicographer most effectively is to compare his remarks in the preface with those in his *Plan of a Dictionary*, published eight years before. The *Plan* is no longer in print, although it can be found in such out-of-print volumes as the 1825 *Works of Samuel Johnson* and Mona Wilson's *Johnson: Prose and Poetry*. The difference in tone and expectation between the pieces makes it clear that something happened to Johnson in the course of his work on the *Dictionary*. In the *Plan*, the fledgling lexicographer sets out a bold, coherent, and confident statement of methodology and intention, which appears to have been severely qualified and challenged by empirical linguistic evidence during the eight intervening years before the preface was written. To examine this change enables the student to uncover central problems of language and lexicography and the more generalized issues related by Johnson to the struggle of life itself.

To illuminate Johnson's general and central shift of attitude, students can examine his confident description, in the *Plan* (pars. 42–53), of his system for providing multiple definitions for words (Reddick). Johnson planned to arrange the definitions of words with multiple meanings under the following categories: (1) the natural or primitive sense, (2) the consequential or accidental, (3) the metaphorical, (4) the poetical, (5) the familiar, (6) the burlesque, and (7) the peculiar sense as used by a great author (the literarily unique). The "primitive" sense that Johnson privileges concerns etymology: it is that meaning closest to the etymon, or etymological root. The other usages are etymologically tied to the original, primitive meaning. In this respect, Johnson's systematic approach for determining multiple definitions was the most thoroughly connected with etymology of any English lexicographer.

At the inception of his work, Johnson saw etymology as the means for establishing the "true" meaning of any word. Students can be asked whether they agree with such a standard. If so, how would they implement it? If not, what would theirs be? In the words of Nathan Bailey, Johnson's lexicographical predecessor, the purpose of etymology is to show "the Original of Words, in order to fix their true Meaning and Signification" (in the preface to Bailey's *Etymological English Dictionary*). In Johnson's preface, however, written after the completion of his work, his confidence in etymology for determining and establishing a logical, systematic relation of meanings has obviously diminished. Here (pars. 49 and 50) he is defensive in his discussion of multiple definitions. "In every word of extensive use," he acknowledges,

> it was requisite to mark the progress of its meaning, and show by what gradations of intermediate sense it has passed from its primitive to its remote and accidental signification; so that every foregoing explanation should tend to that which follows, and the series be regularly concatenated from the first notion to the last.
>
> This is specious [i.e., attractive], but not always practicable; kindred senses may be so interwoven, that the perplexity cannot be disentangled, nor any reason be assigned why one should be ranged before the other. . . .

Here and in the lines that follow, it should be clear to the student that Johnson has not simply lessened his regard for etymology as the determinant of meaning but abandoned his structure for determining meaning on the basis of etymology as unreliable and insufficient (see also the comical quotations ironically illustrating his entry for *etymology*). Instead, he has begun to rely on the empirical evidence contained in the writings from which he borrows illustrations.

Students, in other words, can discover for themselves Johnson's abandonment of predetermined structures for establishing meaning, the most important aspect of any dictionary. This discovery is crucial for understanding both his entire lexicographic enterprise as it eventually took shape and his attitude to the language itself, as well as the development of lexicography. It is often asked of Johnson (and of dictionary makers in general) whether he was attempting to "fix" or "freeze" the language — that is, to establish a correct standard of meaning and usage and proscribe deviations from this standard. He originally desired and intended to do so, but his experience with what he calls "the boundless chaos of a living speech" (par. 28) taught him the futility of such efforts (see esp. pars. 84 and 85, "Of the event of this work . . ."). Though regretting the powerlessness of the lexicographer, he switched from a fixed structure of definition and assessment to one based on usage. And what is pedagogically exciting about this discovery is that students can experience it as a practical and commonsensical issue, as is often the case with Johnson, rather than as an abstract one. Johnson's scheme of "correctness" just didn't work, so he was forced to change it.

To what, then, did Johnson turn to establish his definitions? we can ask the students. How was he able to proceed? How would *you* proceed, given the task? we might ask them. The answer concerning Johnson, as one can find both in the preface and, more important, in the word list itself, is that he turned to the quotations he was gathering to allow *them* to establish the definitions. Thus, in the end, Johnson's *Dictionary* became the first to rely to a large extent on a criterion of word *usage*, written usage, for establishing meaning. As they approach Johnson's entries, students will read the definitions, appropriately, as products of the quotation or quotations beneath, the direct result of Johnson's own reading and of his critical response to the passage.

As we move from the preface to the body of the *Dictionary* itself, then, what happens when students try to "read" the *Dictionary*? How is the task done? In the first place, access to texts is not always easy, of course. (Longman has recently issued a facsimile of the first edition in two volumes. Other texts include the reprint of the first edition by AMS Press and Times Books, and the reprint of the fourth edition by the Librairie du Liban. Donald Greene prints several pages from a later quarto edition in the Oxford Authors *Samuel Johnson*. If possible, students should be given the opportunity to see and dip into the actual folio volumes.) A student should spend some time reading through sections of the *Dictionary*, trying to get a sense of the text and the way one might consult it, both then and now. Are the lexicographer's skepticism and acknowledgment of relative failure, which they have encountered in the preface, evidenced in the word list and entries? In this work — a dictionary, representing authority in the most obvious way — is there evidence of authorial difficulty under the entries? The students can be challenged with these questions.

As Johnson selected quotations, his first criterion was that they provide clear illustrations of specific meanings of individual words. In fact, as we have seen, his definitions eventually grew out of his encounters with these words in printed texts. He claimed other responsibilities for their selection as well, however — moral, philosophical, aesthetic, and technical, in particular (par. 94). But what happens to Johnson's authority in the *Dictionary* when he incorporates hundreds of borrowed quotations as (his word) "authorities"? Whereas we may say that the dictionary's authority is then based on something of a consensus of literary writers, we must acknowledge that Johnson's own authoritative voice is rendered less distinguishable by the presence of many others. The issue of authority is complicated, especially in a work in which the "authorities" have moral, aesthetic, and other responsibilities beyond the strictly linguistic. The passages retain at least an echo of their previous context, whether or not Johnson wished it, of which the user is reminded to a greater or lesser extent by the completeness and specificity of the attribution. Students can find quotations throughout the pages that illustrate this problem or phenomenon.

Is a quotation from *Hamlet*, for instance, to be read as a "simple" illustration of one sense of a word, as proof that the word exists, or as making a political, moral, or religious statement? or several statements at once? And what of the familiarity of the student, or any user, with the play *Hamlet*, which is then brought in as a part of the experience of the *Dictionary*? Where does the illustration of meaning or "authority" stop? One can see the problem especially clearly if one considers the use of the politically controversial figure of Milton, whom Johnson frequently quotes. We might also say that within the new context of the *Dictionary*, the meaning and rhetorical significance of the quotations are further determined through their position with reference to Johnson's definitions, his notes on usage, and the other quotations. Context, in other words, both prior and present, is all; this is the primary reason that we should be very careful to avoid the impression that students can simply isolate what Johnson "says" in his *Dictionary* by extracting quotations from it as aphorisms or by tying them together into themes. A quotation embodies or carries overtones or meanings, whether political, moral, or other, from its previous context, which Johnson was sometimes able to use but not always able to control or determine. In its new context within the *Dictionary*, a quotation seldom functions simply as a passive example of usage, whether or not Johnson intended that it should, and it establishes other meanings, allusions, or suggestions in relation to the rest of the entry Johnson constructs and to its previous context.

Furthermore, an unavoidable opposition exists between Johnson's definitions and his quotations. The former are produced by a drive for exactness, accuracy, and delimitation, but the latter reveal the complexities, and the wide possibilities of signification, of the rhetoric of poets, philosophers, preachers, and other writers. The lexicographer attempts to restrict the meaning of the word in a particular usage, yet the quoted text remains alive with other possibilities. One might ask students to determine from a given quotation the definition of a word as used. The result should illustrate the difficulty of the task and Johnson's remarkable critical ability to determine meaning, as well as the problem of affixing a single meaning to a single usage. This is an aspect of the linguistic struggle within the text, an unresolvable tension resulting from the play of two opposing impulses, that students can discover for themselves. Students might also consider whether Johnson's frequent quoting of lengthy passages, in which he allows the literary voice to spill over from the usual word-etymology-definition-illustration formula, does not actually obscure the exemplificatory purpose of the passage (see, for example, the entry for *investment*).

These complications, I believe, are the most important reasons that the work retains its vitality for us and for our students: Johnson's work is not simply a monumental dictionary, a milestone of lexicography, an inert collection of quotations providing a history of language use, or a collection of Johnson's ideas and themes covering various topics. It is a living literary and critical text, with tensions and dialogues actively engaged under each entry. It is instructive, in my experience, to help students see the *Dictionary* as a text representing and even encompassing a struggle, with language in general and with differing discourses under entries in particular. One way to accomplish this is to have students make some of the decisions that Johnson had to make in the construction of his work. Such a demystification of the "monumental" allows our students to invade the imposing folios of Johnson's *Dictionary*, to break through the air of "monumental impersonality," in Raymond Williams's terms (18), of such huge dictionaries and appreciate the work as the triumph of the spirit, and of linguistic and critical struggle, that it is.

The Jenyns Review:
"Leibnitian Reasoning" on Trial
Thomas F. Bonnell

"What might cause Johnson to become so zealous in this review?" Well might Donald Eddy ask (93). Soame Jenyns's *A Free Inquiry into the Nature and Origin of Evil* (1757) elicited from Johnson not just a penetrating review but a deeply felt response. It was an unlikely reaction, perhaps, since Jenyns's reputation as a wit led many to suspect him of irony (Rompkey 33). Jenyns's work touched a nerve, however, producing what Boswell declared to be "Johnson's most exquisite critical essay" (*Life* 1: 315, ed. Hill and Powell). The Jenyns review, a compact and lively intellectual exercise, works very well as a first reading of Johnson, for it introduces students to his acuity and forcefulness as well as a cross-section of topics that characteristically were of deep interest to the moralist.

Since no general eighteenth-century anthology reprints the full text of the review, instructors will need to put a copy on library reserve. It can be found in *Samuel Johnson*, edited by Donald Greene (Oxford ed.), and in facsimile in Richard B. Schwartz, *Samuel Johnson and the Problem of Evil*. To acquaint the class with Jenyns's work is the first step in teaching the review. One approach is to assign reports to a handful of students, each of whom reads part of the *Free Inquiry* and summarizes its argument in class. The virtue of this method, as it assumes that a report will be required of every student over the term, is in getting the class to venture off the syllabus into lesser-traveled regions of eighteenth-century thought. A second approach is to include on the syllabus Pope's *Essay on Man*. The Jenyns review works well in tandem with the *Essay*, for Johnson used the occasion to unmask Pope's theodicy long before attacking such "Leibnitian reasoning" in his Life of Pope (*Lives* 3: 243, ed. Hill). The benefit of this approach, aside from simpler logistics, is that the whole class will need to grapple with the crucial ideas. If neither alternative is possible, one can resort to lecture or rely on Johnson's excerpts of Jenyns, which adequately convey the method and purpose of the book.

As a brief check, here is what students should find in the *Free Inquiry*. Jenyns embarks on an "abstruse speculation" to determine "Whence came Evil?" In solving this puzzle, he will "ascertain the moral Characteristic of God," for on that "solid foundation" alone can "any rational system of Ethics be built." He asserts (he does *not* ascertain) that God possesses "infinite Power, joined to infinite Wisdom and Goodness" (2–3, 10). How "Evils of any sort could have a place in the works of an omnipotent and good Being" Jenyns acknowledges to be an "incomprehensible paradox" — yet it is a "wonderful paradox" rationally consistent with "the analogy of every thing around us" (14, 15, 5, 13). Since everywhere pain is mixed with pleasure, since "every picture must be composed of various colours, and of light and shade," such variegation must be "the very essence of all created things," not to be prevented "unless by not creating them at all" (26). So it is with the universe, formed on principles of a "just subordination," with all parts perfect in kind but necessarily different. "Omnipotence cannot work contradictions, it can only effect all possible things" (26, 14).

What then was God's choice? Jenyns reformulates the "best of all possible worlds" of Leibniz: "[I]n every possible method of ordering, disposing, and framing the universal system of things, such numberless inconveniences might necessarily arise, that all that infinite Power and Wisdom could do, was to make choice of that method, which was attended with the least and fewest." If things look awry in "the very small part of the universal System that lies within the reach of our imperfect capacities," we can only trust that the world could not have been otherwise "without the loss of some superior Good" (16–17, 19, 15). Jenyns's argument consists of six letters that "divide Evils into their different Species" (20), here listed with the corresponding paragraph numbers in Johnson's review: 1. On Evil in General (1–4), 2. On Evils of Imperfection (5–35), 3. On Natural Evils (36–61), 4. On Moral Evils (62–72), 5. On Political Evils (73–75), and 6. On Religious Evils (76–80).

Pope also serves to prepare students for Johnson's review, since his ideas came to be identified with the *Free Inquiry*. Jenyns quotes *An Essay on Man* only twice (1.155–56, 3.27–40), but so central is Pope's influence that the journal *Critical Review* labeled parts of his book as "but a repetition of what Pope, and many other writers, have already taken notice of" (444). Johnson treats the poet as a virtual coauthor of Jenyns's work, often navigating by Popean stars: Jenyns "rejects the Manichean system, . . . and adopts the system of Mr. Pope"; the "second letter . . . is little more than a paraphrase of Pope's epistles"; Jenyns "proceeds to an humble detail of Pope's opinion"; and "[w]e are next entertained with Pope's alleviations of those evils which we are doomed to suffer" (pars. 3, 5, 11, 23). At one point, noting Jenyns's "mere translation of poetry into prose," Johnson wonders, "[H]ow can vanity be gratified by plagiarism or transcription?" (par. 5). A dozen times Johnson invokes Pope, revealing how deeply he implicated the poet in Jenyns's scheme.

To use Pope's philosophical poem efficiently, one may focus on Epistles 1 and 2, to which Jenyns's main ideas can be traced. Time is well spent on the opening verse paragraphs, where students will encounter the difference between empiricism and rationalism. Pope rigs up a test of Lockean epistemology:

> Say first, of God above, or Man below,
> What can we reason, but from what we know?
> Of Man what see we, but his station here,
> From which to reason, or to which refer?
>
> (1.17–20)

Sensory perception serves as a plausible means of knowing "Man below," but knowing "God above" is a tricky matter: "Thro' worlds unnumber'd tho' the God be known, / 'Tis ours to trace him only in our own" (1.21–22). Earthbound empiricists are hampered by their narrow experience, the only remedies for which would be preternatural faculties or extraterrestrial travel:

> He, who thro' vast immensity can pierce,
> See worlds on worlds compose one universe,
> Observe how system into system runs . . .
> May tell why Heav'n has made us as we are.
> But of this frame the bearings, and the ties,
> The strong connections, nice dependencies,
> Gradations just, has thy pervading soul
> Look'd thro?   (1.23–25, 28–32)

Who could accept Pope's taunting challenge? The key verbs ("pierce," "see," "observe," "look") help students to grasp the sensory resources — largely visual — to which Pope's empiricist is limited. If we reason from what we know, and if knowledge comes only by way of our senses, then we are sorely constrained in our ability to comprehend the universe and our place within it.

Or so Pope would have it. Having teased empiricism into disrespect, he lays a rationalist foundation for his poem:

> Of Systems possible, if 'tis confest
> That Wisdom infinite must form the best,
> Where all must full or not coherent be,
> And all that rises, rise in due degree;
> Then, in the scale of reas'ning life, 'tis plain
> There must be . . .   (1.43–48)

"Wisdom infinite" forming "the best" prefigures the deity of Jenyns's theodicy: all-knowing, all-good, and all-powerful. And the phrase "if 'tis confest" crystallizes the rhetorical dilemma: the theodicy fails without a confession of faith, tacit or explicit, that "Wisdom infinite" has created the best of all possible worlds. (Maynard Mack argues to no avail that the passage is hypothetical, simply the mirror extreme of empiricism [527–28], for Pope clings to this presupposition and later in the poem uses similar language — "and this confest" [4.49] — in the parallel sense of "only grant me this.")

Now the class can address the review, starting with the circular reasoning that Johnson deplores. Ostensibly intent to discover the moral character of God, Jenyns settles the matter without investigation, taking for granted, as Johnson excerpts, "[t]hat there is a supreme being, infinitely powerful, wise and benevolent." This move short-circuits Jenyns's argument. Johnson wryly observes that the "present enquiry is then surely made to no purpose," for Jenyns unwittingly accepts as a premise what should have been the work of his conclusion. Johnson sees that the "system seems to be established on a concession which if it be refused cannot be extorted" (pars. 2, 15). For anyone who will not concede Jenyns's "taken for granted" or Pope's "if 'tis confest," God's threefold perfection is a point not to be gained.

At the heart of Jenyns's theodicy lies the scale of being, set forth in the letter designated a "paraphrase of Pope's epistles." To evaluate this characterization, students can compare the pertinent excerpts (pars. 7, 9, 11–13) with Pope's verses, especially 1.233–58 and 3.7–26. Students will more firmly grasp the doctrine of compensation that informs Jenyns's sanguine view of subordination if one adds to Johnson's quotation the final part of the excerpt beginning, "No system can possibly be formed . . ." (par. 9):

> for which reason, in the formation of the Universe, God was obliged, in order to carry on that just subordination so necessary to the very existence of the whole, to create Beings of different ranks; and to bestow on various species of animals, and also on the individuals of the same species, various degrees of understanding, strength, beauty, and perfection; to the comparative want of which advantages we give the names of folly, weakness, deformity, and imperfection, and very unjustly repute them Evils: whereas in truth they are blessings as far as they extend, tho' of an inferior degree.   (26–27)

Here the chalkboard comes in handy. A simple but effective ploy is to depict the "links" in Pope's "chain of being" (1.237–46), inviting the class to situate various species by rank. The constitutive notions of gradation, continuity, and plenitude, laid out long ago by A. O. Lovejoy, are still useful to help students follow Johnson's logic in dismantling the scale of being.

Instructors should ask students to note the three passages that constitute Johnson's demolition (pars. 14–22, 44, 68–70). Such circling back was to Eddy a sign of disorganization; he saw no need to mimic "the repetition and lack of structure in Jenyns' book" (93). Students can be asked what purpose, if any, is served by the repetition. Johnson himself pleads Jenyns's organization as an excuse. That the scale of being, however absurd, underpins so many of Jenyns's arguments makes it necessary for Johnson to undermine it repeatedly: "I am obliged to renew the mention whenever a new argument is made to rest upon it." What drives Johnson to combat the idea resolutely is not Jenyns so much as Pope, for, he writes, it was a "notion to which Pope has given some importance by adopting it, and of which I have therefore endeavoured to show the uncertainty and inconsistency" (pars. 68, 44). To the extent that the idea enjoyed a limited currency (Hudson 113), Johnson blamed Pope's authority. Had Jenyns not stood on ground consecrated by the *Essay on Man*, the review might have been less zealous.

Thus far students will have been introduced to a Johnson of a keenly logical cast of mind. But the essay reveals a wide range of thought and variety of stylistic address. Students will relish what Donald Greene (*Samuel Johnson* 96–97, Twayne ed.) has described as Johnson's "magnificent invective" and "brutality of satire" in response to Jenyns's attempt to explain away all social and economic ills. His reasoning reminds Johnson of Pope's "alleviations of those evils which we are doomed to suffer" (par. 23). Teachers can refer to the verses in which some "strange comfort" is said to attend "on ev'ry state":

> The fool is happy that he knows no more . . .
> The poor contents him with the care of Heav'n.
> See the blind beggar dance, the cripple sing,
> The sot a hero, lunatic a king;
> The starving chemist in his golden views
> Supremely blest, the poet in his muse.
>
> (2.264, 266–70)

Poverty, ignorance, starvation, madness — no rupture of the social order is too gross to be accommodated to this anesthetizing doctrine. Sarcasm and brilliant parody are two weapons Johnson wields against such nonsense; yet equally at his command are powers of sober reflection and an empathic grasp of ills suffered by the poor and uneducated, which enable him to write with moving intensity. As Eddy admires, "Johnson's wisdom, common sense, broad experience, and humane compassion are perhaps nowhere displayed to better advantage than in these discussions" (91). Some students, sifting their own views for comparisons, are apt to discover sentiments akin to modern liberal attitudes and the faith in universal education, with its supposed dividend of upward mobility. The anachronism of such parallels should be pointed out, as well as the difficulty in pinning Johnson down. The paragraph beginning "I am always afraid of determining . . ." (par. 32) provides an excellent chance to discuss the wariness of Johnson's analyses and his acute sense of political ambiguity.

The review also introduces students to a range of Johnsonian preoccupations. A project for instructors to try is this: students can count up compliments as well as criticisms in the review. They will tally a dozen passages in which Johnson expresses satisfaction with a thought or an apt characterization. These nods of approval, despite Johnson's impatience with the glaring faults of the *Free Inquiry*, have not received adequate attention. The class will note how cursory some of the praise is and how Johnson often pairs an undercutting remark with his words of applause; yet scrutiny of the list yields a catalog of subjects so close to Johnson's psyche that students will encounter them again and again in their subsequent readings.

On happiness (pars. 7, 38), poverty and toil (pars. 46–47), death and aging (pars. 51–52), and true patriotism (par. 75), what Jenyns says warrants an approving excerpt, including one compliment for "spriteliness of fancy and neatness of diction" (par. 50). So sincere is Johnson's admiration for Jenyns's analysis of virtue and vice that he quotes, at a single stretch, nearly one-fourteenth of the *Free Inquiry* (par. 63). In all, roughly an eighth of Jenyns's text is transplanted into the review with marks of praise. Why salvage all this from the wreckage of a spurious system? Where Jenyns "speaks what every man must approve" (par. 8), he earns a fair hearing. For Johnson, "[t]here are truths which, as they are always necessary, do not grow stale by repetition" (par. 50) and even "may be read with pleasure in the thousandth repetition" (par. 6). If Jenyns hits on one of these precepts, "though not new, [it] well deserves to be transcribed, because it cannot be too frequently impressed" (par. 74).

To clarify the sort of truths to which Johnson refers, teachers might call on Ralph Walker's distinction between coherence theories and correspondence theories of truth. The coherence theorist "holds that for a proposition to be true is for it to cohere with a certain system of beliefs. It is not just that it is true if and only if it coheres with that system; it is that the coherence, and nothing else, is what its truth consists in." A correspondence theory of truth, contrarily, maintains that "truth consists in some kind of correspondence with a reality independent of what may be believed about it"; this principle can lead to a skeptical surrender to the supposed "logical gap between what is believed and what is the case" (2, 3, 13). In answer to skepticism, the coherence theory erases the divide between "methods of discovering about reality and the reality itself." Reality is what our standards of rationality and justification make it (9, 14). Jenyns and Pope, perhaps not fully aware of what they are doing, take up positions within this stronghold. Whatever *is*, is right, not because evil and pain do not exist but because a coherent framework of belief explains why it must be so; partial evil is universal good because this perception is the one warranted within their system of belief.

System, then, is what Jenyns's theodicy is about, a set of mutually entailing premises and deductions or, as Nicholas Hudson puts it, "a massive system of interdependencies between all beings (even on other planets)" (119). This point was as evident to Johnson as to the reader for the *Critical Review*, who lumped Jenyns together with Pope and "his brother system-makers" (444). In four of his initial quotations, Johnson documents how the system is defined (pars. 3, 9, 11). He will allow neither Jenyns nor Pope to resort to universal causes that, by their own admission, cannot be known apart from a divine revelation that neither pretends to consult. "When this author presumes to speak of the universe," Johnson admonishes, "I would advise him a little to distrust his own faculties, however large and comprehensive." The faculty Johnson himself trusts is indicated in his phrase "as far as human eyes can judge." "Life must be seen before it can be known. This author and Pope perhaps never saw the miseries which they imagine thus easy to be borne" (pars. 43, 4, 26). Only where Jenyns puts system aside to describe human life can the correspondence theory of truth be applied to his observations. Only then does Johnson grant a few high marks.

With these issues the class will anticipate a basic aesthetic tenet of Johnson's: the "just representation of general nature." Just representations satisfy the test of correspondence ("just" in its third *Dictionary* sense, "exact; proper; accurate"), but an even higher appeal is made to the consolation a representation can or cannot afford. Students may be asked to consider this remark: "Of poverty and labour he gives just and elegant representations, which yet do not remove the difficulty of the first and fundamental question, though supposing the present state of man necessary, they may supply some motives to content" (par. 45). Accurate representation is not enough. Jenyns offers "nothing that can silence the enquiries of curiosity, or calm the perturbations of doubt" (par. 42). The book does not measure up to either criterion in Johnson's telling paraphrase of Horace's dictum: "The only end of writing is to enable the readers better to enjoy life, or better to endure it" (par. 60).

Such glimpses of Johnson's intellectual struggle are one reason the review is interesting to teach. Given a few minutes, the class will find several confessions of doubt, beginning with the mood of biblical resignation at the opening, where Johnson predicts the futility of attempting to unknot a "perplexity which has entangled the speculatists of all ages, and which must always continue while *we see* but *in part*" (par. 1). Though he chides Jenyns for not recognizing his limitations as a writer, Johnson claims no absolute superiority ("I do not mean to reproach this author for not knowing . . ." [par. 56]; "The author has indeed engaged in a disquisition in which we need not wonder if he fails . . ." [par. 66]). Instead, he confesses his own failure — "the chain of nature I have often considered, but always left the inquiry in doubt and uncertainty" (par. 14) — and assumes the voice of a weary companion voyager: "In our passage through the boundless ocean of disquisition we often take fogs for land, and after having long toiled to approach them find, instead of repose and harbours, new storms of objection and fluctuations of uncertainty" (par. 22).

"[W]e are devolved back into dark ignorance" (par. 80). This is no very triumphant conclusion. At hour's end one can pose a question for review and further thought. Why could Johnson not accept the Jenyns-Pope system, when as a Christian he would have assented to their entailing premise, the irreproachable character of God? (See Hudson 115–17.) What Johnson craved is what Jenyns and Pope presumed to offer: an easing of spiritual anxiety. It is a testimony to Johnson's courage that he rejected their anodyne.

Teaching A *Journey to the Western Islands of Scotland*

Thomas Jemielity

Teaching Samuel Johnson's *Journey to the Western Islands of Scotland* presents problems and challenges not encountered with more familiar items in the Johnsonian repertoire.[1] In this essay, however, I suggest ways in which the very problems can be turned into pedagogical opportunities. For example, if Johnson is the stereotypical, even the archetypal, urbanite, why did he have a lifelong desire to see this forsaken spot? Second, students who may instinctively associate Johnson with *The Vanity of Human Wishes*, *Rasselas*, or the *Lives of the Poets* might consider his special fondness for the *Journey*, his conviction that it embodied something unique in his writings, and his disappointment in its apparently poor sale. Students can be sent on a search-and-find mission that will reinforce the rarity of finding the *Journey* anthologized or even mentioned in standard literary and Johnsonian texts. The *Journey*'s dim contemporary presence sharply contrasts with the controversial quality of the book in its own time, which helped to make it one of Johnson's best-selling items, even if the ruthless pirating of the *Journey* prevented him from profiting much from the controversies it engendered. Students should also be asked how and why the *Journey* generated such a storm. Was it too sympathetic to the Highlanders, many of whom had sought, in 1745–46, forcibly to restore the Stuarts to the British throne? Was it, as some Scots thought, too unsympathetic and ungenerous in its comments? And, finally, what of the penetration of Johnson's account? He insisted that the Highlands afforded a unique opportunity for visiting and analyzing a different society, virtually autonomous, within the British Isles. Yet it was changing as he traveled, because the British government was seeking to eliminate, by force, its distinctive and assumedly rebellious character. Late-twentieth-century students should have little difficulty understanding and sympathizing with a minority culture that is losing its identity as the result of punitive measures directed against it. Such awareness should lead students to consider Johnson's own attitude toward this once distinctive social order. What sympathies, biases, and limitations emerge in his commentary on the Scottish Highlands? These are the pedagogical themes that are my concern in this essay and that reflect my own teaching of Johnson's *Journey to the Western Islands*.

Johnson's Lifelong Fascination with the Scottish Highlands

A subject of fascination from his boyhood, the Western Islands of Scotland pique Samuel Johnson's vigorous curiosity from the moment his father places into his hands Martin Martin's early-eighteenth-century account of the islands, where Martin himself lived. In 1773, after ten years of friendship, the personal circumstances of Johnson and James Boswell, an indispensable major domo for the trip, prove mutually conducive to the "ramble," as Johnson calls it four years later while admitting that the experience still "hangs upon [his] imagination." In his seventy-second year, he asks Boswell: "Shall we ever have another frolick like our journey to the Hebrides?" (*Letters* 2: 184, 456, nos. 528, 756, ed. Chapman). In his first considerable literary chore, after all, the 1735 translation of Father Jerome Lobo's *Voyage to Abyssinia*, Johnson claims that the "eminent degree of curiosity" that distinguishes "a generous and elevated mind" is never "more agreeably or usefully employed, than in examining the laws and customs of foreign nations" (cited in Boswell, *Life* 64, ed. Chapman). By 1760, before his pension makes possible the travel so frequent in his last three decades, his voracious appetite for travel books leads him to claim, in *Idler* no. 97, that they often deny the "gratification" readers look for in them. How characteristic of Johnson to consider travel as intellectual inquiry and pursuit and to speak of it as satisfaction and enjoyment, as appetite and desire. How revealing of him, too, to make his recollections of the Highland ramble a supreme pièce de résistance in the menus considered by his boundless imaginative appetite. This dish was no common fare, such as could be found throughout eighteenth-century Europe, where only language, accent, or title might change within the same basic experience. Boswell himself discovers this in the mid-1760s. Legal studies in Utrecht were hardly equal to a trip to Brobdingnag. What Johnson seeks, on the contrary, is that relatively unknown, semiautonomous nation, the Highlands and Western Islands of Scotland, which, in 1773, is feeling the effects of Britain's determination to preclude another Highland-based, pro-Stuart uprising like that which had alarmed the British in 1715 and especially in 1745. Charlie, Bonny Prince Charlie, was not the darling of the English. So at sixty-three Johnson travels north to spend just over seven weeks in this remote region of Britain. Clearly, he does not share Daniel Defoe's dismissive view of these islands, which the latter neither visited nor wanted to visit, for how likely was it that "any person whose business was mere curiosity and diversion should either be at the expense, or run the risk of such a hazardous passage where there was so little worth observation to be found" (Defoe 669)? "*Mere* curiosity and diversion"? Not for Johnson. So he rambles among the Hebrides. No inns, no towns for that matter, no carriage, sometimes on horse, sometimes on foot, much rain, travel plans interrupted or delayed or changed by the weather, accommodations sometimes unavailable and hastily arranged at the last minute, danger, but admitted only once — when Johnson thinks of this journey, he calls it a "ramble" and a "frolick"! Any admirer of Johnson who owns an American Express card must be profoundly embarrassed.

The Journey's *Popularity, Then and Now*

What does disappoint Johnson is the apparently poor sale of the *Journey to the Western Islands*. True, in the weeks just following its publication in January 1775, the booksellers assure him that "the sale is sufficiently quick" (*Letters* 2: 12, no. 360) and, true, the four thousand copies of the first two editions are sold. In his last known comment on the matter, however, in the spring of 1778, Johnson registers disappointment that the book has not achieved "a great sale" because "in that book [he has] told the world a great deal that they did not know before" (*Life* 973).

Were Johnson still unshaken about the originality and value of the *Journey*, its virtual absence in texts designed to introduce undergraduates to British literature, to the eighteenth century, or to Johnson himself would add to his disappointment. Early editions of *The Norton Anthology of English Literature*, that "presence that will not be put by," mention the *Journey* only in the introductory comments on Boswell, whose "lively and entertaining" *Hebrides Journal* is contrasted, in the fifth edition, with Johnson's "thoughtful account of the way people live in the Hebrides" (Abrams et al. 2434). Was it a Scots editor, perhaps, who had described the *Journey* in the fourth edition as a "sober and unflattering account"? (Abrams et al., 2378). Since Boswell disappears in the Major Authors Edition of the *Norton*, the *Journey* disappears with him.

More concentrated courses on Johnson will find only a few pages in Bertrand Bronson's anthology, and all devoted to Ossian; none at all in the Frank Brady–W. K. Wimsatt *Johnson*; but a generous sampling in Donald Greene's Oxford anthology, which also summarizes the omissions. *Idler* no. 97 appears neither in Bronson nor in Greene. Walter Jackson Bate's anthology of over eighty periodical essays (*Selected Essays*), in whole or in part, doesn't include it either. Available paperback editions of the entire *Journey*, by Allan Wendt (Houghton) and Peter Levi (Penguin), continue the long-standing practice of having Johnson share his covers with Boswell. The comments that follow might suggest more advantageous possibilities for using not Boswell but *Rasselas* as a pedagogical companion piece to the *Journey*: travel as fiction and travel as fact, both embodying what Johnson insists — in a letter from the Highlands — to be the purpose of travel: "to regulate imagination by reality, and instead of thinking things as they may be, to see them as they are" (*Letters* 1: 359, no. 326).

Since "no man but a blockhead ever wrote, except for money" (*Life* 731), Johnson's assurance about the sales potential of the *Journey* proves sound, even if he profits little from the book. For in authorized and pirated editions, in abridgments, and in translations, the *Journey* sees print twenty-five times in its first fifty years, an appearance on the average, in some form, once every two years. What Johnson perceives is the interest to be generated by an account of a place that has forcefully impressed itself on the forefront of British consciousness at least twice in his lifetime, a place about which considerable ignorance and perhaps fear still subsists, and a place about which any analysis and evaluation can scarcely avoid, as Johnson does not, some of the most controversial questions of the time. This is the deeply appetitive lure of the Western Islands of Scotland in 1773; this, I affirm, is the pedagogical lure of those islands for the late-twentieth-century student. Left with only its language and its poverty, the one assaulted and the other slowly abating, the society of the Highlands of Scotland is unfamiliar, suspect, and subject, an embattled minority within Great Britain, trying to maintain its identity in the face of a frightened, vindictive, unsympathetic, and highly assured English-speaking colossus to the south and in the face of indifferent and acquiescing Highlanders and Lowlanders themselves welcoming and speeding forced assimilation because they can point to advantages that seem hard to deny. Is it any wonder that the *Journey* is pirated in London in the very year of its publication? The Highlands are a hot item.

Johnson as a Social Historian

In a comparatively brief work, Johnson provides, first of all, a fairly comprehensive analysis of a society that he is perhaps the first to deem worthy of a philosopher's curiosity. As Mary Lascelles points out, although "men better informed on Scottish antiquities" can easily correct Johnson on details of Highland life, none can match Johnson's "grasp of the whole: the pattern of a peculiar way of life, its causes and effects" ("Some Reflections" 8–9). Johnson wants his readers to understand not only how these people are but, more so, why they are this way. When he first interrupts the apparently topographical arrangement of his material, the section "The Highlands" affords not so much a general picture of how Highlanders live but an analysis of why they live as they do. He pursues at some length, consequently, the effect on them as mountain people of their isolation and remoteness and the effect on them of the now forced and more apparent intermingling. His lengthy commentary on the Isle of Skye takes up the economic, social, and cultural features of Highland society, the three major themes of his analysis; a concern with Highland economy emerges in the remarks about its agriculture: the condition of land, animals, harvest, and weather. Industry and commerce in the islands, meager though they are, engage Johnson's interest. He describes, analyzes, estimates, and proposes remedies for the widespread emigration of the Highlanders, which reached its peak during the 1770s. Understanding the feudal and patriarchal principles at the heart of the old Highland order, he reconstructs the old system of chief, steward, and people. Keenly interested in how they secure education, in what they believe, in the superstitions they admit, Johnson is led by curiosity, perhaps credulity as well, to consider whether at least a few of the Highlanders might lay claim to the extrasensory power of the second sight. He wants to know how they worship and with what facility they can do so. And he wants to determine, finally, what basis, if any, underlies the claim of a centuries-old literary tradition in a region scarcely literate. In particular, is Ossian real or a fraud? The apparently topographical arrangement of Johnson's material yields at various places in the *Journey* to reflections about what he has seen, to an emphasis, in his own words, on "notions" rather than "facts" (*Letters* 1: 409, no. 357). The arrangement of material under place names, however, also fixes Johnson's commentary hardheadedly and empirically in the place in which these people live. Johnson reminds others, as he reminds himself, that whatever is said about the Highlands cannot ignore the conditions in which the Highlanders carry on the task and the burden of living. This brief but comprehensive analysis of an entire social order should enable students to see Johnson as a philosopher examining a culture, aware of its contemporary life, making clear what he admires and deplores, and seeking always to expand the bases of his knowledge and the cogency of his judgments about the Highlanders.

Johnson and the Changing Highlands

As Johnson travels, however, the Penal Laws of 1747 have had a visible effect on the old order. The Highlanders may not bear arms or even wear the plaid. The abolition of the heritable jurisdiction of the lairds has struck at the heart of the feudal and patriarchal order. The effect is "perhaps never a change of national manners so quick, so great, and so general, as that which has operated in the Highlands, by the last conquest [i.e., 1746], and the subsequent laws." Johnson admits that he and Boswell "came thither too late to see what [they] expected, a people of peculiar appearance, and a *system* [my emphasis] of antiquated life" (Johnson and Boswell 73, ed. Levi). Johnson, consequently, re-creates that old order, in one of the major imaginative achievements of the *Journey*. From his own preparation, from inquiry, on those rare occasions when it proved trustworthy, and from edifices, "standing or ruined," that he calls "the chief records of an illiterate nation" (85), Johnson calls up images of a violent, unattractive past. However compelling to his curiosity, Johnson's regret about the disappearance of the old Highlands is a philosopher's lament, not a traveler's sentimentality. Here in the *Journey* is perhaps Johnson's most sustained engagement in anti-pastoral. The old Highlands, he insists, lived in the "continual expectation of hostilities," under "unprincipled and unenlightened chiefs," none of whom was likely to prove "a nice resolver" of disputes (100). True, in the old Highland order, Johnson recognizes an admirable spirit: "Every man was a soldier, who partook of national confidence and interested himself in national honour. To lose this spirit," he concedes, "is to lose what no small advantage will compensate." But Johnson immediately counters any possibility of banal nostalgia by pointing out that "a man, who places honour only in successful violence, is a very troublesome and pernicious animal in time of peace," a comment Swiftian in its severity. The social consequences are baneful: "All the friendship in such a life can be only a confederacy of invasion, or alliance of defence. The strong must flourish by force, and the weak subsist by stratagem" (99). "The system of insular subordination, . . . having little variety, cannot afford much delight in the view, nor long detain the mind in contemplation" (97).

Of the emerging Highlands, Johnson admits he can form "no settled notion" because "the state of life, which has hitherto been purely pastoral, begins now to be a little variegated with commerce." Although he assumes a wiser and more equitable justice in the new order and the gradual abatement of poverty as one of the not "unpleasing consequences of subjection," a profounder skepticism ponders "whether a great nation ought to be totally commercial" (97, 74, 99). The stability that comes with the blood tie finds no counterpart in commerce, where interest is the guiding principle. Almost a century before Thomas Carlyle warns, in *Past and Present*, about "cash payment" as "the sole nexus of man with man," Johnson writes, in his "Introduction to the Political State of Great Britain":

> No mercantile man, or mercantile nation, has any friendship but for money, and alliance between them will last no longer, than their common safety, or common profit is endangered; no longer than they have an enemy, who threatens to take from each more than either can steal from the other.   (*Political Writings* 143–44)

The indemnification of the lairds for their loss of jurisdiction, a compensation Johnson defends as just, nonetheless acquaints them with "perhaps a sum greater than most of them has ever possessed" and the resulting "thirst for riches" metamorphoses some of the chiefs into landlords. While ordinary Highlanders are expected to struggle in an unpromising landscape and brutal climate, with inefficient and makeshift tools, the example of their too often absent lairds hardly encourages them to withstand the pressures to emigrate. Perhaps rents should be limited. Perhaps Highlanders might be indulged the plaid. Perhaps, in areas difficult of access to courts, lairds might occasionally exercise their old power. If the new order is to improve, however, the Highlands need, above all, chiefs like Donald Maclean, young laird of Col, who learns improvements at first hand and works with his people to show them what can be done. His islanders, Johnson points out, "have not yet learned to be weary of their heath and rocks, but attend their agriculture and their dairies, without listening to American seducements." The heartfelt praise for this young man, whose death in a crossing among the islands in 1774 the *Journey* laments, sharply contrasts with the laconic, emotionally suppressed remark about Alexander Macdonald, laird of Skye, and his wife, who greet Johnson as he lands. These two were "preparing to leave the island and reside at Edinburgh" (Johnson and Boswell 128, 67). Hardly an encouraging omen at the very start of the island tour.

So Johnson vigorously enters the debate and demonstrates throughout, but tough-mindedly, the "tenderness toward conquered and invaded peoples" that Donald Greene finds "one of the most consistent of his political attitudes" (Greene, "Johnson's Contributions"). Trees can be planted; agriculture and its implements can be somewhat improved; lairds can develop and maintain an interest in their people; tacksmen or stewards can impart civility, not just collect rent; and government can thoughtfully and sensitively attend to the needs of these once-rebellious people and not idiotically content itself with creating "a wilderness" where there was once "an insurrection." Such a Lagado-like scheme "argues no great profundity of politicks" (Johnson and Boswell 103).

Throughout this engagement, further, a complex of emotions emerges: deep gratitude for hospitality, wonder at civility in remote places, admiration for the daily heroism of Highlanders, irritation and frustration with their inaccuracy and lack of curiosity, an ongoing bantering with Boswell about the supposed inferiority of Scotland, simple fatigue, willful refusal to speculate on some matters, yet satisfyingly indulged fancy about what the isolated traveler might have encountered here in the past. Yes, indeed, a "frolick" and a "ramble."

Braidwood's Academy: An Image of the Highlands?

Although Johnson passes over the month's return and stay in the Lowlands with a brevity that accentuates his interest in island society, he nevertheless presents as the very last "subject of philosophical curiosity" Thomas Braidwood's college of the deaf and dumb, who are taught to speak, read, write, and practice arithmetic. A touching, characteristic, and thoroughly appropriate final image emerges in these five paragraphs. The lexicographer, turned sixty-four on the islands, perhaps in his brown traveling suit, writes a multiplication problem on the slate for a young deaf girl. She successfully meets the challenge but fails to add the two lines. Too "easy an operation," Johnson surmises. He points to the place where the figures should appear, and she readily obliges with the sum.

Much of Johnson's attitude to the Highlands is epitomized in this scene: the deep sympathy evoked by hardship that seems almost natural and inevitable; an equally deep desire for amelioration, with an insistence that claims of improvement must be tested; a conviction, seen in the young deaf girl's readiness, that human beings cannot but be satisfied to discover that even apparently insurmountable obstacles are capable of some remedy. That powerful, outgoing imagination so characteristic of Samuel Johnson in *A*

Journey to the Western Islands of Scotland impels him to the picture that frames a good deal of this tale in the next-to-last paragraph:

> It was pleasing to see one of the most desperate of human calamities capable of so much help: whatever enlarges hope, will exalt courage; after having seen the deaf taught arithmetick, who would be afraid to cultivate the Hebrides?   (Johnson and Boswell 152)

NOTE

[1]The J. D. Fleeman edition is the definitive version of Johnson's *Journey*, with much helpful information about this highly allusive book. Although its cost makes it an unlikely choice for a text, any teacher of the *Journey* should be familiar with the Fleeman.

Johnson and the Limits of Biography:
Teaching the *Life of Savage*
Charles H. Hinnant

I teach the *Life of Savage* in two contexts: undergraduate survey courses on the late eighteenth century and graduate seminars on Johnson and his circle. I usually begin by discussing the difficulties most readers have had in estimating Johnson's achievement in the *Life*. Hence I start by observing that Johnson has invariably been praised for his interpretive power, for his ability to organize the sensational events of Savage's life into a coherent narrative. A useful point to make is that from this essentially "literary" stance, the *Life of Savage* has often been described in generic terms: as an ironic comedy or satire, as a Greek tragedy or medieval morality play. Yet one must also note that allowances have always been made for Johnson's apparent haste in composition, for his obvious reluctance to consult all the available records. At issue in the discussion is whether this clash between literary and historical priorities has not created a deep-seated uncertainty about the value of the work. One must thus ask whether Johnson's honesty, acumen, and unwillingness to suppress unfavorable details about his friend's life are sufficient to counter a powerful empiricist creed that would effectively consign such virtues to an older rhetorical tradition of moralizing biography.

What the discussion dwells on at this point is the question of biography as posed by two conflicting perspectives, each with a legitimate claim to the student's attention. To help the class in grasping the implications of these two perspectives, I suggest that the goal of an exhaustive historical or biographical investigation assumes as its normative limit an exact correspondence between text and reality, language and life. To challenge that goal, however, is to suspend the canon of mimetic realism at precisely that point where it seeks to contest the notion that the biography is an inescapably rhetorical or literary genre. But what the discussion leads up to is the possibility that the *Life of Savage* may not be comprehended by either of these two perspectives. In exploring this possibility with students, I introduce an unsigned letter to the *Gentleman's Magazine*, in which Johnson, conceding that "others may have the same design," goes on to inform its editor:

> As it is not credible that they can obtain the same materials, it must be expected that they will supply from invention the want of intelligence, and that under the title of the life of Savage they will publish only a novel filled with romantic adventures and imaginary amours. You may therefore perhaps gratify the lovers of truth and wit by giving me leave to inform them in your magazine, that my account will be published in 8vo by Mr. *Roberts* in *Warwick Lane*.
>
> (qtd. in Clifford, *Young Sam Johnson* 274)

Students are struck by the way Johnson obviously seeks in this notice to preempt the kind of fictionalized life that is exemplified in a "history" like Daniel Defoe's *Roxana*. In *Roxana*, which Benjamin Boyce identified as a remote precursor of Johnson's biography, whatever core of fact may exist is submerged in the fictive expansion of the putative biographer or editor (578–80). Students recognize that in Johnson's announced life, by contrast, the proportional emphasis on fact and fiction, "intelligence" and "invention," is reversed, yet the life is still expected to appeal to "lovers" of both "truth and wit." This amounts to an implicit rhetoric of biography, an assumption that fiction is still involved, yet a fiction that derives from the "real," not the "imaginary."

In a more advanced class, students will not fail to observe that Johnson's brief notice is a typically combative and charged piece of writing. It sets out not only to announce the *Life* but to treat it as a primer for readers, a test case of what a responsible biography ought to be when measured against the "romantic" falsifications of fictionalized lives. Yet there is no suggestion, as some students will point out, that this conception of responsibility embraces the ideal of an exhaustive investigation of available sources. No doubt this was partly a matter of contingent historical circumstance. Johnson, I emphasize in the discussion, was legitimately anxious to capitalize on the notoriety of Savage's life. But I also suggest that there is a more general lesson to be drawn, one that raises a question about the relation between fact and fiction, life and character. In the mid–eighteenth century the term *character* was still related to its founding sense as a "mark" or stylus; hence I introduce a citation from the *Dictionary* in which Johnson gives as one of his definitions of the word *character*, "mark" or "stamp." As such, a character is etymologically analogous to a portrait that represents yet does not pretend to exhaust or merge with its subject. Rather than seek to plumb the depths of the human heart or understand the ways the mind works, biographers restrict themselves to the kind of writing that confines itself to the visible, phenomenal surface—that is to say, the characters—of their subjects. I draw the class's attention to the possibility that the effect of this limitation might well be evident throughout the *Life*; it might be discerned, for example, in such comments as Johnson's observation that Savage "appeared to think himself born to be supported by others and dispensed from all Necessity of providing for himself" (Wilson 116). The restriction of the commentary to what Savage "appeared to think" imposes a limit on what can be discovered through investigation and analysis. What this constraint encourages the class to recognize is the notion of a kind of biography that refuses, as it were, to take responsibility for what cannot be inferred from common knowledge, immediately available sources, and eyewitness observation.

At this point I suggest that the rigorously self-imposed limits of Johnsonian biography are masked, to a certain extent, by its style. Throughout the *Life of Savage*, as students readily perceive, Johnson adopts the unitary language of cultural authority. The central features of this language — its stability, universality, and generality — impel it to a consistent level of generic abstraction: its most important words, its common nouns, are almost always the names of ideas. Yet a careful discussion of specific passages reveals that these nouns are never meant to match up with things in a simple one-to-one correspondence. Rather, they demarcate open concepts that acquire particular and sometimes conflicting meanings in different contexts. When I ask students to look at the phrase Johnson uses to describe the trait that "constituted" the "character" of Sir Richard Steele — "the Ardour of Benevolence" (47) — they note that it was obviously meant to be seen as a commonplace. But the most advanced members of the class also recognize that the ambiguity embodied in this commonplace — it can refer either to selfless generosity or to narcissistic delusion — aptly reflects the ambiguity of Steele's intentions toward Savage, or of Savage's uncertainty concerning what to expect from Steele. In a similar manner, Johnson's account of Aaron Hill's "Generosity" to Savage is lent urgency by the qualifying phrase "when Mr. Savage's Necessities returned" (54), yet the term "Necessities" leaves the class guessing as to whether Johnson is referring to the imperatives of self-preservation that he describes so vividly elsewhere or to the compulsive displays of luxury that contributed so much to Savage's decline.

A few students may object that these shifting connotations are remote from the issue of factual reliability. Yet I answer that what is at stake here is the question of the difference between the Johnsonian life and the modern ideal of an empirically researched and naturalistically conceived biography. The commonsense notion of a stable, continuous, and immanent link between world and text, the real and the written, is inextricably related to the notion of a stable and unitary subject. In arguing for this essentially conventional view of naturalistic biography, I suggest that its leading figures might well be shown to change or develop according to some hypothesis but can never be seen to differ from themselves. Their character traits are manifest and susceptible to a comprehensive and authoritative interpretation. It is precisely this notion of a unitary subject, I contend, that the *Life of Savage* appears to contest. By insisting on a gap between character and life, by passing over numerous opportunities for an omniscient reading, Johnson effectively challenges the wholeness, the integrity of the natural; fissures appear between the biological and the cultural; between the probable (i.e., what is naturalistically motivated) and the strange (what Johnson refers to as "the barbarous"). Perhaps the easiest way to help students grasp this point is to encourage them to see that in the *Life of Savage* the textual gulf between the general and the particular cannot be separated from the psychic gulf between the decorous and the disruptive — the "barbarous," or "monstrous," emerges beyond the realm of propriety, beyond the realm, that is, of natural affection or rational self-interest.

The most obvious example of the monstrous in the *Life of Savage*, as all students recognize, is the countess of Macclesfield. To give the class a sense of just what is at stake, I usually cite John Wain's observation that Johnson "makes no attempt to probe the Countess's psychology" (*Samuel Johnson* 112), in conjunction with such comments in the text as Johnson's insistence that "it is not easy to discover what Motives could be found to over-balance that natural Affection of a Parent" (42). Barbarity, as the proscribed other of that self-sufficient "natural Affection," the suppressed and disturbing physiognomy of perversion and difference, is what gives the *Life of Savage* its depth and dimension. What I try to encourage students to recognize, however, is that the countess of Macclesfield is only the most extreme form of this kind of otherness. Thus I suggest that the contrast between the unitary, the natural, and the self-sufficient, on the one hand, and the divided, the unnatural, and the parasitic, on the other, may well occur in various guises throughout the *Life of Savage*: as the inexplicable disparity between promise and performance, wisdom and folly, candor and duplicity, generosity and insolence. To emphasize this point, I ask the class to discuss the behavior of several of Savage's patrons — behavior that, as Johnson portrays it, is marked by an irrational doubleness and cruelty. Of Sir Richard Steele, Johnson observes that "though he was always lavish of future Bounties . . . [he] was very seldom able to keep his Promises, or execute his own Intentions" (48). Of Lord Tyrconnel, Johnson notes that after his rupture with Savage, he "came with a number of Attendants, that did no Honour to his Courage, to beat him at a Coffee-House" (76). Even in the character of Savage himself, Johnson describes "Compassion" as somehow coexisting with "Resentment" (62).

I believe that the norm by which the difference between the proper and the barbarous is measured in the *Life of Savage* is most simply explained to students as aristocratic, heroic, and stoic. This norm is formally enunciated through the opposition between master and slave, aristocrat and plebeian, that guides Johnson's assessment of Savage's character. To support this contention, I ask the class to examine Johnson's judgment that Savage was "the Slave of every Passion that happened to be excited by the Presence of its Object, and that Slavery to his Passions reciprocally produced a Life irregular and dissipated. He was not Master of his own Motions, nor could promise any thing for the next Day" (116). After discussing this passage, students have no difficulty in understanding how Johnson implicitly attributes Savage's own anomalous, hybrid state, which is reflected in his unstable amalgam of hauteur and servility, to a confusion of class roles, to his apprenticeship as a shoemaker and subsequent discovery, by accident, of his aristocratic birth (45). I suggest that, for Johnson, Savage's precarious social identity may have been most poignantly dramatized in the emerging London publishing world where he is seen as rejecting every opportunity to achieve independence by earning his living and thus breaking free of the sycophancy of the patronage system. To Savage — who, Johnson sadly observes, never "endeavoured even to secure the Profits which his Writings might have afforded him" (116) — the support he received from others was a right, while his "insolence" toward his patrons was an inevitable concomitant of his aristocratic pretensions.

One way to help students understand the difference between the natural and the monstrous is to suggest that the distinction might have a sexual as well as a social dimension. I point out that male disablement is perhaps the most striking form of the loss of self-mastery, the alienation of authority, that provides the standard by which Johnson evaluates Savage's life. Although Johnson never explicitly ascribes Savage's weakness to his birth, he accepts Savage's explanation of his predicament, portraying the countess of Macclesfield as an unnatural and castrating female, a vengeful mother whose own authority, significantly enough, is compromised and ungrounded, the product of adultery and illegitimacy. Savage's father was the notorious earl of Rivers, but students will point out that the earl is depicted in the *Life* as a weak and ineffectual figure whose early death only confirms his essential lack of authority. By contrast, one can draw attention to numerous passages in which the countess's power is seen as having an undeniable effect on Savage's attempts to achieve manhood. In one place, Johnson declares, "she never left any Expedient untried, by which he might be cut off from the Possibility of supporting Life." The countess is portrayed not merely as the enemy of her son but also as the robber of the phallus, the symbol of power and authority. "The punishment which our Laws inflict upon those Parents who murder their Infants is well known," Johnson asserts, but he then goes on to ask "what Pains can be severe enough for her who forebears to destroy him only to inflict sharper Miseries upon him; who prolongs his Life only to make it miserable" (51).

Admittedly, students are not always convinced by this sort of explanation, which they sometimes interpret in literal terms, but they can be persuaded that the effects of Savage's upbringing are more complicated than first appears. One can observe that Savage's estrangement from his patrimony is such that none of the chain of substitute parental figures who seek to help him — whether his nurse, Mrs. Oldfield, and the queen, on the one hand, or Steele, Wilkes, and Lord Tyrconnel, on the other — can overcome it. The "universal Accusation of Ingratitude" leveled against Savage leaves little doubt about the failure of these surrogate figures. To function as substitutes, they must resemble in some essential way the original parents they replace, but these originals are themselves substitutes, illegitimate and perverse replicas of the "natural" parents Savage never had. In the more advanced class, I suggest that these surrogates are related to a fundamental structure of substitution, a structure that is internalized in Savage's mind in an endless chain of images and replicas. As Johnson describes it, Savage

proceeded throughout his Life to tread the same Steps on the same Circle; always applauding his past Conduct, or at least forgetting it,

> to amuse himself with Phantoms of Happiness, which were dancing
> before him; and willingly turned his Eyes from the Light of Reason,
> when it would have discovered the Illusion, and shewn him, what
> he never wished to see, his real State.   (79)

The only way that temporal succession can be introduced into this circle
of illusion is through a series of lurching shifts between hope and disappointment: Savage, Johnson observes, "spent his Life between Want and Plenty,
or, what was yet worse, between Beggary and Extravagance; for as whatever
he received was the Gift of Chance, which might as well favour him at
one Time as another, he was tempted to squander what he had, because
he always hoped to be immediately supplied" (63).

This ubiquity of the substitute does not mean that there is no difference
between "Want" and "Plenty," between "Beggary" and "Extravagance."
These extremes are crucial and play a prominent part in the external events
of Savage's life. But many students will detect the logic of substitution even
in Savage's most prosperous moments. They will recognize that his celebrated wit and charm, for instance, are the dispossessed son's substitute for
the power he lacks and the weapons he cannot bear; the resentment, insolence, and cruelty that he sometimes displays are the resort of the impotent
and plebeian. One can suggest that even in his "Fortitude," his ability to
suffer well, there may be something of that quality of servility and self-
delusion that for Johnson characterizes his "unhappy Life." Savage is not
self-sufficient. He is, rather, divided, self-consciously and theatrically seeking through his conversational "Arts" and ingratiating manner to represent
himself to others in an effort to recover a "Splendor" that has been irretriev-
ably lost. His attempt to recapture the patrimony he has been denied never
really succeeds; his constant borrowing is not the practice of the aristocrat
but a mimicry of it, his lamentation at "the Misery of living at the Tables
of other Men" undercut by his readiness to "comply with every Invitation"
(67, 97). Some students may observe that, by exposing this mimicry, Johnson is seeking to discourage any temptation to view Savage as a truly heroic
figure of baffling complexity or romantic appeal. If Johnson accepts Savage's
story of his birth, he rejects Savage's illusion of a nobly suffering mind. In
Johnson's account, Savage emerges as a second-rate version, a derelict imitation of the aristocratic grandeur that no amount of effort will enable him
to reproduce.

All this, one needs to emphasize, is not to suggest that the *Life of Savage*
is informed by the debunking irony of fictions like Fielding's *Jonathan Wild*.
Classroom discussion may suggest a horizon of interpretation in the
narrative, but it is a horizon that remains latent rather than explicit. In
the calculated ambiguities of Johnson's biography, the central characters
are allowed to retain their aura as enigmas, their resistance to the kind of interpretation that would reduce matters of conjecture to a satirical coherence.

What is at issue is the notion that "the innumerable Mixtures of Vice and Virtue, which distinguish one character from another" (64) can be wholly accounted for in rational terms, or that motivation, as the paradigm of rational inference, cannot be subject to concealment and mystification. The purpose of the discussion is to suggest that Johnson's *Life* regularly focuses on events where such inferences begin to break down, where obscure compulsions elude rational understanding, and where time and human error turn out to place insuperable obstacles in the path of any simple explanation of human behavior.

This approach has the advantage of encouraging students to recognize that the ambiguities of Johnson's narrative may not be an accident but a constituent part of its structure. While Johnson's biography enjoins skepticism about the possibilities of an overarching analysis of motives, it also eschews the kind of imaginative expansion embodied in the conventions of direct discourse and dialogue. For this reason I insist that it is a falsification of Johnson's intentions to view him as displaying a cavalier disregard for the virtues of truth telling and accuracy. What the *Life* brings out, rather, is a Lockean sense of the limits of human understanding, its subjection of biography to constraints that no amount of research will be able to bypass. Indeed, students may point out that Johnson's account becomes most literary, most rhetorical, at precisely those moments where biography comes up against the limits of finite observation. It is in the lacunae created by Johnson's reluctance to probe the countess's motives, by his unwillingness to offer a comprehensive explanation of Savage's willful dissipation of his talents, that one can detect the generation of the fictional, the literary. By seeking to approach Johnson's *Life* from the vantage point of its own self-imposed restraints, students can arrive at a reading that is richer and more complex than the one we have sometimes been accustomed to present in the classroom.

Teaching the *Lives of the Poets*

Lawrence Lipking

There are many reasons not to teach the *Lives of the Poets*. It is a long and miscellaneous work, without a plot, and much of it deals with poets whom students have never heard of and may never hear of again. The texts are hard to get; anthologies tend to offer mere snippets, distorting the *Lives* as a whole, and fuller collections keep going out of print. Moreover, even the best editions (G. B. Hill's, or the volumes forthcoming in the Yale *Johnson*) leave out one vital part of the original context. Johnson intended his work to be published not by itself but rather as *Prefaces, Biographical and Critical, to the Works of the English Poets*, in fifty-six volumes. Hence the student who reads the *Lives* without reading the poems to which it refers will be introduced to Johnson but not to what Johnson introduces. Such a reader has to take critical judgments on faith, which is never a good idea and was certainly not the author's. Nor does this end the teacher's problems. The *Lives* assumes a great deal of background information about English history, religion, and politics (how many modern readers know what party Addison belonged to?), as well as versification (how many modern readers know how to scan?). And because Johnson himself sometimes got facts wrong, an additional burden is placed on the teacher. Should Johnson's account of Milton, for instance, be allowed to stand uncorrected, or should the teacher use class time to set it straight? There are no easy answers to such questions, and no one ought to expect teaching the *Lives* to be easy.

All these may be good excuses. But a teacher who uses them to dodge the *Lives of the Poets* will be cheating students of an experience they can hardly find anywhere else. The *Lives* is one of the essential works of English biography and criticism, as well as the culmination of Johnson's lifelong interest in poets and poetry. It also offers something more: a way of looking at life. Johnson judges each person, as he judges each work of art, on the basis of *principles*—fundamental truths or grounds of conduct—and the *Lives* shows how such principles work in practice. Not many students have been exposed to this perspective; or, if they have, they may associate it with empty moralizing rather than with the fierce intelligence that shines through Johnson's prose. The *Lives* is a storehouse of living principles, tested against the way that some notable writers have actually behaved. Some students still find these examples useful; Johnsonians spring up spontaneously in the classroom. But even those who resist can be challenged to define their own principles. What gives a life meaning, and how is it to be judged?

It follows that, in my teaching, I try to engage students in the workings of Johnson's mind—not so much *what* he thought on specific topics as *how* he arrived at his judgments. To experience the *Lives* from this perspective requires a little time. Rather than leap from one famous highlight to another — the definition of wit in the Life of Cowley, the demolition of *Lycidas*, the comparison of Dryden with Pope, the final deference to the common reader in the Life of Gray — I recommend starting with the whole of one life. Ideally the subject might be a major poet such as Milton, Dryden, or Pope, with whose work students may already have some acquaintance. But lesser lives can also be instructive. For instance, I have had good luck with the little piece on Shenstone, who spent his life in making his gardens look good ("nothing raised his indignation more than to ask if there were any fishes in his water"), and teachers who are fond of Butler or Thomson will not go wrong by looking at their lives first. The point to stress is not the size of the career but how Johnson perceives it.

Take some time also to watch Johnson's use of his sources. I do not mean that students and teachers have to investigate all earlier biographies (Sprat's *Cowley* and Richardson's *Milton*), though doing this can be a valuable exercise. But the story of a life can be told in many different ways, depending on who is telling it and for what purpose. This point fascinates students. Many of them have never seriously considered that the authoritative stories they read, in encyclopedias or scandal sheets, present only one possible interpretation of the evidence. Johnson lets us look over his shoulder. He tends to be candid about how little he knows and how often he speculates. With rare exceptions, a few previous accounts supply him with all his facts, and his own contribution as a biographer consists of weighing that evidence. How much can it be trusted? To some extent this question motivates the *Lives*. The first, on Cowley, begins by reproaching Sprat for offering much panegyric and few details, and a similar quarrel with sources comes up again and again. Students should be encouraged to question Johnson too. Could we use the same facts to tell another story? That was Johnson's own assignment, and it can be assigned to students as well.

Sometimes the *Lives* makes the conflict of stories explicit. For instance, the Life of Edmund ("Rag") Smith (one of my favorites, and an interesting parallel to *Life of Savage*) quotes a long and friendly biographical sketch of Smith by Oldisworth, goes over the facts again with a more skeptical eye, and ends with a tribute to Gilbert Walmsley, who in his youth had been a friend to Smith and in his old age a friend to Johnson. If this biography is notable for its personal warmth, it also stands out for multiple perspectives, as if Smith were judged not only by different sets of values but by different generations. Students notice this. A similar effect occurs in the Life of Swift. After a harsh section on the "depravity of intellect" that invented the Yahoos, Johnson continues, "I have here given the character of Swift as he exhibits himself to my perception; but now let another be heard who knew him better" (3: 63, ed. Hill), and gives the last word to Swift's friend Delany. A comparison of these clashing perceptions can reveal the basic problem of writing a life, the problem of knowing the truth about another person. Johnson does not keep that problem a secret; he involves his readers in it. The doubt that students may feel about the truth of the *Lives* is not the least important lesson they learn.

The search for truth goes deeper than sources, however. The *Lives* consistently probes the relation between the public record of the poet's life, which includes not only his writings and the testimony of acquaintances but his reputation among readers, and the private acts or habits that expose the state of his soul. Johnson seldom trusts appearances. A poet like Pope may claim that his letters to friends "flowed warm from the heart," but according to Johnson, "very few can boast of hearts which they dare lay open to themselves, and of which, by whatever accident exposed, they do not shun a distinct and continued view; and certainly what we hide from ourselves we do not shew to our friends" (3: 207). This skepticism about the sincerity of fine sentiments, and especially about poets who profess to be honest and content, colors all the *Lives*. Some students may find Johnson's attitudes not only skeptical but brutal. He does not believe that Cowley was really in love, that Milton really stood for liberty (at least for other people), or that any pastoral poet was ever really happy in the country. Hence an innocent question—What does Johnson think of this poet?—is likely to provoke some hot responses: He hated him! He thought he was a fake! This is an opportunity for the teacher, a chance to turn the discussion from personal reactions—Johnson's like or dislike of poets, students' like or dislike of Johnson—to the grounds for such judgments. The *Lives* does stir strong feelings, whether of sympathy or discomfort. But those feelings ought to lead back to matters of principle.

In this respect the *Lives* is easy to teach. Wherever one picks it up, principles load the page. Of the fifteen paragraphs devoted to the earl of Halifax, for example, the last five all treat one topic, the compliments that other poets paid him in return for being paid. Johnson refuses to condemn them:

> To charge all unmerited praise with the guilt of flattery, and to suppose that the encomiast always knows and feels the falsehood of his assertions, is surely to discover great ignorance of human nature and human life. In determinations depending not on rules, but on experience and comparison, judgement is always in some degree subject to affection. Very near to admiration is the wish to admire.   (2: 47)

This passage typifies Johnson's mode of analysis. It begins with a stock response, contempt for flatterers, and gradually refines and deepens it through an appeal to principles of human nature. Johnson judges works of art, as he judges people, not according to abstract rules but in the light of "experience and comparison"; we cannot take the measure of poems or human beings except by comparing them with others. At the same time, however, the particular example counts for less than the lesson it instills. *All* of us are well disposed toward those who do us good. What students think about Halifax does not matter. What matters is what they might learn about themselves. In a good discussion of such a passage, therefore, students will reflect on their own experience. Do they flatter their friends — or perhaps their teachers? Should they feel guilty about it? Reading the *Lives* may not make a student wise, but it ought to convey some sense of what wisdom sounds like.

When I teach the *Lives*, I encourage this sort of reflection by asking students not only to comment on Johnson's statements of principle but to formulate their own. One written exercise that usually works is a brief imitation of the method of the *Lives*, in which a few biographical facts about a friend or acquaintance lead to some pronouncement on human nature. Read these lessons aloud. Although students do not write them well (the exercise should not be graded!), they do enjoy pretending to be moralists, and they are quite able to tell the difference between each other's efforts and Johnson's. It is fascinating to hear how authentic the true voice of wisdom sounds when compared with impersonations. Almost everyone learns to recognize that voice.

To teach individual passages, however, is not to teach the *Lives*. Johnson also asks more comprehensive questions about each poet's life: What has it added up to? Was it well spent? These questions include the poet's conduct in his personal affairs as well as his artistic achievement. As a critic, Johnson wants to know how much the poet has contributed to English poetry as a whole or to our notions of what poetry might be. As a moralist, he wants to know whether the poet has made the best possible use of his talents. This view of life pervades Johnson's work (before students read the *Lives*, a brief study of *Rambler* no. 60 and "On the Death of Dr. Robert Levet" will be useful). The idea that each of us will be judged in the long run not by our native abilities but by how well we employ them may seem familiar. We tell students, after all, that grades register how hard they have worked, not just how smart they are; and coaches tell athletes that doing one's best, not winning, is the object of the game. But to a culture obsessed with test scores, winning, and worldly success, often these sentiments savor of hypocrisy. The *Lives* sets forth the principle in practice. It pictures human life as a series of choices or perpetual tests of character. As much as Johnson values genius, he values more the exercise of free will, the person who actively lives up to his or her principles.

The emphasis on life as a series of choices, or what might be called "character" rather than "personality," is something I always try to teach. One good place to introduce this point of view is Johnson's criticism of Pope's theory of the "ruling passion," the doctrine that a single innate and irresistible desire governs each life. This doctrine simplifies the writing of biographies, since the story of any one person always amounts to one passion (as in Pope's own *Characters of Men and Women*). But Johnson detests the theory. It is not only false, since desires and their objects both keep changing, but also pernicious:

> Its tendency is to produce the belief of a kind of moral predestination
> or overruling principle which cannot be resisted: he that admits it is
> prepared to comply with every desire that caprice or opportunity shall
> excite, and to flatter himself that he submits only to the lawful
> dominion of Nature in obeying the resistless authority of his "ruling
> Passion."   (3: 174)

Such a belief would render free will and a moral life impossible. The *Lives*
resists this implication at every point. It holds each poet responsible for everything he does, whether killing a king or writing a sonnet, and assesses each
life as the sum of such decisions.

For the student also, therefore, the *Lives* is a test. To read it properly
means to enter into its choices, constantly to ask, "What would I have done
in this situation?" Students like to moralize at a distance. It is the teacher's
job, as it was Johnson's, to close that distance, by prompting students to
imagine themselves in someone else's place. To think of oneself as a potential Savage, Milton, or Rochester may be unnerving. It may also be the key
to developing a moral imagination.

Some teachers might consider this emphasis on character a distraction
from the main business of the *Lives*, its criticism of poetry. Johnson lives
on, after all, as a model critic. But the critical sections, like the biographical,
concentrate on performance — not on what a poet is but on what he does.
The unsparing exercise of judgment that Johnson brings to people he also
brings to poems. This perspective can open the eyes of students. Many of
them, when they do not associate criticism with mere carping, suppose it
to be a justification or apology for works of art. In the classroom, teachers
generally treat the poem as finished and faultless; to read it well means to
understand how everything works, the organic whole. That is not how Johnson sees poems. He regards them, rather, as the result of many choices, some
good, some bad, like any product of human ingenuity. Virtues are balanced
by faults, and nobody is perfect. The mystery of the creative act does not
impress Johnson. Instead he views poets as people doing a job, with more
or less care. The special dignity of writing poetry consists of only this: no
job is harder to do well.

Thus Johnson holds poems accountable for the same good conduct he
expects from people: moral intelligence, learning, common sense, correct
diction and grammar, a lack of pretensions, honest effort, and a proper
concern for the literal truth. If the pastoral form of *Lycidas* is "easy, vulgar,
and therefore disgusting" (1: 163), that is what he will call it (though all
three adjectives need to be glossed by Johnson's *Dictionary*). Some students
may be appalled at first. But most will be delighted, too, not least because
he voices their own suspicions and doubts. No one who reads the criticism
of the *Lives* should ever believe again that poetry does not have to make
sense. No critic is more teachable than Johnson on the attack. Teachers and

students may want to defend the metaphysical poets, the *Essay on Man*, or Gray's odes, but the challenge will force them to sharpen their critical tools — above all, to pay attention to exactly what the text says. When Johnson talks against a poem, everyone listens. "*Paradise Lost* is one of the books which the reader admires and lays down, and forgets to take up again. None ever wished it longer than it is" (1: 183). Students usually find this frankness thrilling. A teacher will want to set it in context (Johnson pitied readers who could not respond to "that wonderful performance *Paradise Lost*" [1: 188]) but not to explain it away. The example of a critic who holds to his standards and speaks his mind can last for a lifetime.

When students read the whole of a major life, one question almost always comes up: What connects the biography with the criticism, or the person with the poet? This question motivates literary biographies in general. It becomes acute in the *Lives*, however, because Johnson deliberately keeps the two sections apart. The Life of Milton poses the problem most sharply. Johnson warns against the bad example of Milton's politics and character and then honors his greatness as a poet. Should we conclude that life is one thing and poetry is another? Most scholars do not think so; they point to the sublime ambition that characterizes Milton in his private and public life as well as his art and find subtle relations between the states of mind that lead to inciting a revolution or to writing an epic. But a teacher need not settle the issue. Students can learn a good deal from arguing the point among themselves. It will help them to reexamine many of the assumptions or stereotypes about poets: that they always write about themselves (even when they seem to be writing about "Satan"), that they are unworldly and unqualified for running a government or a household, that they sacrifice everything to their art, and that geniuses are different from, and better than, other people. The *Lives* supplies ammunition to shoot down such assumptions. In addition, the central section, or "intellectual character" (Johnson's main structural innovation), builds a bridge between biography and criticism. Close reading of those sections shows how Johnson links the story of a poet's life with his individual performances by focusing on powers of mind. My own favorite, in this respect, is the Life of Dryden, in which a middle section deals with the poet's criticism and the final section with his poetic character. A student who has already read Dryden will profit most from these sections, but they are so fine that they can stand alone.

These characterizations of each poet's powers of mind — Milton's sublimity, Dryden's active curiosity, Pope's poetical prudence — also illuminate Johnson's project as a whole. Not many teachers will assign all the *Lives*, yet every reader should keep in view that the work is more than the sum of its parts. The question of what each poet has accomplished suggests the larger question of what poets have done collectively to show what human beings are capable of doing; the sequence of poets implies a history of English poetry during the previous century; and the judgments of the choices people make, their grand hopes and usual comedowns, amount to an anatomy of life. The *Lives* exemplifies a certain way of looking at poetry, not as a realm superior to ordinary life but as an activity that brings out the worst and the best in people who are like ourselves — or sometimes what we might want to be. It is written to be of use to the common reader and the common student. Hence, after the book is closed, it can work as a starting place for further discussion. Critics have been arguing with Johnson for more than two centuries. To give students the means of taking part in that argument should be the special pleasure of teaching the *Lives*.

Rasselas in an Eighteenth-Century Novels Course

Melvyn New

While I was editing the volume in this series dedicated to *Tristram Shandy*, my attention was most particularly drawn to the severe division in our curricula between eighteenth-century "novel" courses and "literature" courses. Indeed, I quoted one respondent to the *Tristram* questionnaire who indicated that in her long career she was never "allowed" to teach *Tristram Shandy* because she was the "eighteenth-century specialist" rather than the "novel specialist." I then went on to contemplate briefly that work's fate in the light of such territorial gerrymandering:

> Overwhelmingly, it is taught in courses in the eighteenth-century novel, where instructors progress with amazing uniformity from Defoe through Fielding and Richardson (or Richardson and Fielding) to Sterne, and then on to Smollett. One eventually becomes known, fairly or unfairly, by the company one keeps. When students encounter *Tristram Shandy* after *Pamela* or *Clarissa*, it is obviously a very different book to them than when they come to the work after *Joseph Andrews*. Their expectations, what they look for, what questions they ask, how they expect characters to behave and stories to unfold — all must be affected by the reading they have done in the immediate past (and, to be sure, over the years as well). How much more, then, would these expectations be changed if *Tristram Shandy* were read immediately after *A Tale of a Tub*, *Gulliver's Travels*, or *The Dunciad*? Or after *Rasselas*, published in the same year as the first two volumes of *Tristram*; or *Candide*, which, even though it *cannot* be taught in a course in *English* literature, was also published in 1759? The year 1759 might be thought of, indeed, as an annus mirabilis of works of fiction that are not very responsive to treatment as "novels." (19)

We do not have so rigid a separation of responsibilities at the University of Florida, and I teach both our novels course and our age of Johnson course on occasion; I include *Rasselas* in each. In the "literature" course, we usually come to it after reading *Rambler* and *Idler* essays, the *Life of Savage*, and *The Vanity of Human Wishes* — and before Boswell's *London Journal*, to which it makes a splendid foil. It is worth noting that because we have eighteenth-century literature divided into two independent courses (Age of Dryden and Pope, Age of Johnson), we teach Johnson and his age to students who, for the most part, have not read Dryden, Bunyan, Swift, Pope, or Addison except perhaps in a sophomore survey course. Hence the context for *Rasselas* in the age of Johnson course is primarily Johnson's own canon; what emerges is the masterly philosophical work of a writer intent on reconciling Judeo-Christian moralism with the recalcitrant facts of life, a noble example of wisdom literature that, like *Vanity*, traces its roots to the preacher of Ecclesiastes. I regard this achievement most highly, and indeed have often quoted the wisdom of *Rasselas* to both my sons and my students when a good dose of pragmatism (as opposed to dogmatism — mine or their own) seemed called for; I know of few works (of any century) in which a more honest, more sympathetic, more useful encounter with the adolescent experience of living takes place (I do realize, of course, that Rasselas is not a teenager — like Boswell of the *Journal*, he is simply acting like one) and am still reactionary enough to believe that such encounters have something to do with undergraduate education.

Nevertheless, I have found myself in recent years interested as well in a somewhat different *Rasselas*, namely the one we discuss in the novels course, and I concentrate on that work for the remainder of this brief account. I teach *Rasselas* after Defoe, Richardson, and Fielding and before Sterne, Goldsmith, Smollett, and Austen. We come to it in the very middle of the fifteen-week semester, and in several ways it is the fulcrum I use to turn the course from the past to the present, from my concern to provide secular students the necessary background for understanding *Robinson Crusoe*, *Tom Jones*, and *Clarissa*, to a quite opposite concern to forestall their too ready absorption of what they read (especially *Tristram Shandy* and *Emma*) into their twentieth-century experience, their tendency to turn every author into "one of us." It is indeed to *Lord Jim* that I turn to begin a discussion of *Rasselas*, both because of Conrad's leitmotif "*he was one of us*" and, even more apropos of *Rasselas*, because of that wonderful passage in which Stein gives his own version of Johnsonian wisdom: "A man that is born falls into a dream like a man who falls into the sea. If he tries to climb out into the air as inexperienced people endeavour to do, he drowns — *nicht wahr?* . . . No! I tell you! The way is to the destructive element submit yourself, and with the exertions of your hands and feet in the water make the deep, deep sea keep you up. So if you ask me — how to be?" (153). A passage from Gide's *The Counterfeiters* also helps set the stage; it occurs toward the end of the novel when the young Bernard asks Edouard how to choose a goal, a way of life: "I have none to give you. You can only find counsel in yourself; you can only learn how you ought to live by living" (327).

For students already strongly predisposed to *Rasselas* — it is, after all, 1,200 pages shorter than *Clarissa* — the idea that the situation of *Rasselas* is echoed by Conrad and Gide is inviting. They have surely noticed for themselves several ways (besides length) in which *Rasselas* differs from our previous readings, and the invocation of modern writers offers them a peg on which this sense of difference might depend. Three observations in particular may occur to students who have read Defoe, Fielding, and Richardson immediately before reading Johnson's fiction. First, Johnson has little interest in the concrete details of action, place, and psychology (sentiment), the very details that not only give *Clarissa* its infinitely patient surface (as opposed to the episodic impatience of *Rasselas*) but also provided the focus of our attention for all three authors as we explored emerging differences between the way they shaped experience and the way it had been shaped by earlier allegorists and romance writers (whom we do not read but whose formal characteristics must be discussed in the first seven weeks of the term). Second, the lack of a conclusion contradicts the stress we found on a sense of ending in Defoe, Richardson, and Fielding. Third, *Rasselas* lacks any overt Christian content, while Christianity is a pervasive presence in the earlier fictions. Reading *Rasselas* alongside *Lord Jim* and *The Counterfeiters*, alongside the intense moral problematics of these representative modern novels, seems to establish just the proper context for envisioning the major shift of direction we have been anticipating. Indeed, *Rasselas* may well herald the arrival of precisely the mode of secular narrative that I have all along been positing as a straw figure. Where in *Robinson Crusoe* or *Clarissa* the question of "how to live," one's "choice of life," is never really in doubt (trust God and follow the commandments), one searches in vain in *Rasselas* for either Scripture or Church; Rasselas appears to be as deliberately separated from England (and the comforts of "home-truths") as is Lord Jim. Similarly, while from the very beginning we understand that *Tom Jones* will resolve itself in marriage, emblematic of an orderly (and ordered) universe, the discussion of marriage in *Rasselas* is filled with almost as many doubts, confusions, and contradictions as in Gide's work. Marriage cannot serve as an emblem of order, nor is any other sacramental resolution of the quest offered (although the princess's "choice of eternity" comes close [*History of Rasselas* 149, Penguin ed.]).

However, the first observation, Johnson's lack of interest in detail, seems to work against the other two (lack of conclusion and lack of Christian content), at least insofar as I have suggested to the class that a strong emphasis on particularity accompanied the development of a new mode of fiction designed to mirror forth a world in which truth consisted of facts and figures rather than sacraments. Imlac's "enthusiastic fit" in chapter 10, I believe, argues directly against this concept of particularized truth, as indeed does Johnson's prose style in general, so different is its aphoristic quality from the far less formal styles of Defoe and Richardson or the elaborate parodic voices of Fielding. Where the styles of these authors might best be understood as instruments for exploring alternatives and accumulations, Johnson's careful use of the most formal rhetorical devices labors to sweep aside every alternative but its own assertion. If the world of *Rasselas* is secular and problematic, its narrator, nonetheless, speaking now through one character, now through another, enforces our consent to numerous generalizations with what appears to be sacramental confidence. Take, for example, this string of "truths":

> This is often the fate of long consideration; he does nothing who endeavours to do more than is allowed to humanity. Flatter not yourself

with contrarieties of pleasure. Of the blessings set before you make your choice, and be content. No man can taste the fruits of autumn while he is delighting his scent with the flowers of the spring; no man can, at the same time, fill his cup from the source and from the mouth of the Nile.   (103)

The authentication of experience, which in the earlier fictions of the course was seen to oscillate between a weakening ideology and a strengthening pragmatism, is accomplished in *Rasselas* by what appears to be dogmatic pragmatism: experience is the sole test of truth, but human experience worth relating is everywhere the same. At one level, we resist so paradoxical a formulation, even while our nods of agreement with every parallel phrase, every balanced clause, reveal our submission to its validity on the level that really matters.

What I have tried to achieve up to now is to reconstruct the approach to *Rasselas* that might emerge among readers whose immediate familiarity with other eighteenth-century authors is limited to Defoe, Fielding, and Richardson. It should be evident, however, that such a reading will not fully coincide with what better-informed commentary says about the work — or even with what students might say who are reading *Rasselas* in the age of Johnson course. Hence, at this point (somewhere during the second of three class periods spent on the work) I introduce the *other* Johnson to the class, to suggest something about the hopes and fears from which the voice of certitude emerges and something, as well, about his criticism of precisely the narratives that have thus far shaped our reading of his work. I might begin with a passage from *Rambler* no. 4 (19 May 1750):

> [W]hile men consider good and evil as springing from the same root, they will spare the one for the sake of the other, and in judging, if not of others at least of themselves, will be apt to estimate their virtues by their vices. To this fatal error all those will contribute who confound the colours of right and wrong, and instead of helping to settle their boundaries, mix them with so much art that no common mind is able to disunite them.   (Greene, *Samuel Johnson* 178, Oxford ed.)

Pointing out that Johnson almost certainly is directing his condemnation toward *Tom Jones*, I ask students to compare *Rambler* no. 4 with these words of Imlac:

> The causes of good and evil . . . are so various and uncertain, so often entangled with each other, so diversified by various relations, and so much subject to accidents which cannot be foreseen, that he who would fix his condition upon incontestable reasons of preference, must live and die inquiring and deliberating.   (77)

It is quite possible to reconcile these two views but even more useful, I believe, to allow them to stand as an indication of an unresolved contradiction, an illustration for students that the "settling of boundaries" is indeed more difficult than totalizing professors usually like to admit.

Simply put, Johnson expects the work of art to convey experience not as it seems to occur — randomly, accidentally, without shape or design — but, rather, as it should occur in an ordered, moral world. Fielding's error (from Johnson's viewpoint), despite characters named Allworthy and Sophia and places named Paradise Hall, despite the conclusion in marriage and the punishment of Blifil, was that he opened too much distance between his narrative and allegory, between a story reflecting the variety, contradiction, and flux of experience and a story reflecting some preconceived order. Yet it is Johnson, not Fielding, who most determinedly rejects fixing the conditions of his fiction on "incontestable reasons of preference" — that is, on the moral equivalent of allegory; and while Fielding ultimately allows his narrative to retreat from uncertainty (although not, I would maintain, his narrative voice), Johnson makes undecidability the bedrock of his own fiction. It would not be unfair to say that Johnson wants other fiction writers to lie but will not tell lies himself.

Unlike Defoe, Richardson, and Fielding, for whom all uncertain events must be brought, by hook and crook, to a morally certain conclusion, Johnson begins with so clear a concept of teleology (indeed, eschatology) that he is able to present all the randomness of experience without any threat at all to his moral vision. The class has experienced this structure of belief once before, while reading *Clarissa,* and during the final class period I concentrate on how the strong belief in immortality allows Johnson — as it did Richardson — to reconcile all human failure and flux without altering the narrative's relation to experience. At this point I confess to the students that I have been deceptively ignoring what I believe is Johnson's strong Christian intent in *Rasselas* — as strong an intent, certainly, as any we have discussed in Defoe or Richardson. I base my comments primarily on Robert G. Walker's fine monograph *Eighteenth-Century Arguments for Immortality and Johnson's* Rasselas, still the best extended examination I know of the context of the work; in particular, I use it to explore the difficult final chapters (45, 47, 48), in which death and the soul are the topics of discussion. Mundane uncertainty and inconclusiveness provide Johnson the evidence he seeks for the necessary existence of certainty and conclusiveness elsewhere; he is not, after all, "one of us" but a believer in "hell-fire everlasting," a reader who sympathized more with Richardson than with Fielding because he perceived accurately enough that Richardson's world was also shaped by a necessary belief in immortality while Fielding's was not. In the course of fiction's development during the eighteenth century (or at any time, obviously), no question is more fundamentally important than that of whether the narrative ends here or hereafter; *Rasselas,* more than any other fiction of the period, forces us to confront that question.

In the classroom, of course, one has time to flesh out these generalities by a closer attention to narrative incidents. One illustration here will have to suffice. If we read *Joseph Andrews* instead of *Tom Jones*, we might look carefully, for example, at Fielding's and Johnson's use of the same trope to celebrate Christian faith over stoicism, the best moral philosophy the classical world can offer (bk. 3, ch. 11, and bk. 4, ch. 8 of *Joseph Andrews* and ch. 18 of *Rasselas*). If we do read *Tom Jones*, however, I like to compare in particular the kidnapping of Pekuah, perhaps the oddest episode in *Rasselas*, with Lady Bellaston's plot to have Sophia raped (bk. 15), which Fielding calls, in anticipation, "the most tragical Matter in our whole History" (796). The framework for analysis is provided largely by Sheldon Sacks's most useful distinction between apologue and novel in *Fiction and the Shape of Belief*, a study behind much of what I teach about *Rasselas* and eighteenth-century fiction in general. I would point out, for instance, that only the most unsophisticated reader fears for Sophia's virtue, that however much we may be involved in accompanying her to a satisfying outcome, we certainly are not concerned about her reaching it. Fielding is simply not going to allow Sophia to be raped or murdered, or Tom to be hanged; the fabric of his fictional world, unlike Richardson's in *Clarissa*, does not allow for irrevocable disasters to befall his heroes. The question, then, is not what dire event will occur but, rather, how it will be prevented. In *Rasselas*, on the contrary, the kidnapping is so unexpected (it is the only novelistic action in the work) that we are momentarily, at least, taken aback and share some of Nekayah's anxiety — not, obviously, her direct concern over Pekuah, who exists for her as a person, but, rather, a concern for a narrative (a world) that has quite suddenly escaped our comprehension. In the light of the text to this point, I do not think we can predict the outcome of this "unexpected misfortune" (109), simply because we have no idea why it occurs; it is "unexpected" in a way that the various "accidents" befalling Sophia and Tom are not. Significantly, Johnson restores equilibrium to both the reader and Nekayah by illustrating how quickly we absorb this "accident" into our reading and our life; we use it to learn something about the impermanence of even the deepest sorrow, the resilient capacities of human nature. Even for Pekuah, it turns out, the "disaster" is a learning experience. This seemingly commonplace narrative situation is quite a difficult and challenging experience for the reader of *Rasselas*, an illustration of the absolute power and authority Johnson retains as an author who can, at any moment, intervene in and disrupt every expectation created by his own orderly world. As such, the incident, in addition to its "moral" about the transience of sorrow, suggests the attributes of that other Author as well, and in a manner perhaps more persuasive than Fielding's special Providence. In *Tom Jones*, virtue is authorized by its escape from misfortunes, in *Rasselas* by its capacity to endure them.

My use of *Rasselas* for teaching the final fictions of the course is perhaps not as direct as with *Tristram*, but Johnson never does disappear from view.

If we move to such subsequent works as *A Sentimental Journey, A Man of Feeling,* or *Humphry Clinker,* for example, I bind them together with the idea of a "modern" venturing forth into the world, a secular and hence open-ended pilgrimage, in contrast to the more closed journeys of *Robinson Crusoe* and *Tom Jones.* In another direction, I have always raised the question of Johnson's presence in fictions by members of his extended circle — *The Vicar of Wakefield,* obviously, but also *The Female Quixote* and *Evelina,* all works I frequently teach in this course. Worldly innocence in conflict with experience and pragmatic observation is one of several common threads running through these fictions. *Rasselas* is particularly useful, I have found, in negotiating the possible ironies of the *Vicar,* which restages the drama of Johnson's work, the argument for immortality based on the disturbing inconclusiveness (and unfairness) of this world. And finally, since I almost always end the course with *Emma,* I cannot resist comparing Hartfield with the happy valley, since in both it is the boredom of perfect security that seems to undergird all endeavor; the novel's dangerous dependence on the expanding middle class — and its children — is surely reflected in that observation.

Teaching Johnson's Critical Writing

Stephen Fix

I teach a course at Williams College called Samuel Johnson and the Literary Tradition. Taken primarily by majors who have already completed a required survey of English literature, this course was originally designed to provide an opportunity to reconsider, from the vantage point of the first serious historian of our literature, the characteristic values and styles of the literary tradition from Shakespeare to Gray. While reading (all in their entirety) and discussing the Preface to Shakespeare and six of the *Lives of the Poets* (Milton, Cowley, Dryden, Pope, Swift, and Gray), students reread some of these poets' works (already familiar to them from the survey course) in order to evaluate Johnson's views and to sharpen their own sense of the achievements that shaped the tradition.

As context for and preface to that discussion, the first third of the course focuses on Johnson's other writing, including the *Life of Savage*, numerous moral and critical essays from the periodicals, *The Vanity of Human Wishes*, *Rasselas*, and the *Plan* and preface to the *Dictionary*. Through these works students come to understand something of the drama and struggle of Johnson's own life as a writer: his delicate negotiation between the demands of morality and the needs of art; his deep brooding on the dangers and virtues of a powerful imagination; his tense argument with himself about the nature of his authorial talents and vocation, which seems to culminate so poignantly in the preface to the *Dictionary*, when he finds himself dreaming "the dreams of a poet doomed at last to wake a lexicographer" (Brady and Wimsatt 291).

As the course has evolved (with essentially the same syllabus) over several years, the difficulties and sympathies Johnson generates have prompted students to shift the primary emphasis more toward the critic himself — more toward an effort to learn about Johnson by knowing what and how he thought about the tradition. Usually against their own expectations, students become absorbed by the hopes and conflicts at the heart of Johnson's own career as a writer, absorbed by the way he experiences and responds to the excitement and turmoil of the creative process. Knowing more about Johnson as a writer, they are prepared to know more about him as a reader and a critic, prepared to move quickly beyond the flat stereotypes of Johnson that his criticism can too easily invite: the harshly judgmental arbiter of taste, the presumptuous dictator of prescriptive rules, the aloof advocate of regularity and correctness. They are ready to hear Johnson's as a more complex voice, one that might speak with sympathetic understanding of the difficulties of writing, the confusions of reading, the varieties of art.

All this preparation helps provide an intellectual framework and vocabulary once we turn to the central texts in Johnson's critical canon.

We explore, of course, the usual variety of issues: the value Johnson did and did not attach to "rules"; the ways in which he sees some point of fixity as a precondition for innovation and change; his belief, first articulated in the moral essays, that the prevalence of some great talent in a life or artistic career implies a corresponding deficiency.

But whatever specific issue engages us, my goal as a teacher is less to persuade students to adopt any particular position about Johnson than to suggest the importance of a certain method of reading and interpreting his criticism. My hope, briefly put, is to instill in them, first, the habit of reading Johnson not just as a critic but as a *writer* of criticism and, second, an awareness that Johnson is engaged in an effort not so much to theorize about literature as to articulate and generalize from his own responses as a reader.

Perhaps I could best explain this not altogether shocking ambition with a story from my own experience as a student. My doctoral dissertation was a study of Johnson's Milton criticism. For months I labored over the Life of Milton, summarizing and schematizing (as only writers of dissertations can) the specific claims Johnson made about Milton and his works. But still I felt distant from the heart of Johnson's real argument; the source and motive of his puzzling alternation between lavish praise and bitter attack seemed elsewhere. When I laid out these frustrations in a conversation with my adviser, he offered a bracing suggestion: try reading the Life of Milton as if it were a novella or poem. Focus less on its prosaic claims and more on the implications of its imagery, diction, and metaphors. Treat it, in other words, not only as a work of criticism but as a work of art.

Even in the wake of recent controversies that have stressed the importance of examining the metaphorical implications of critical language, this way of approaching Johnson is still not entirely obvious or immediately congenial, at least for undergraduates. There is a strong impulse in students of eighteenth-century writing—and of its critical prose particularly—to regard figurative language as decorative language, meant only to enhance and clarify arguments more overtly stated elsewhere in a text. It is thought to drive home rather than carry the point; it might be used by a reader to confirm rather than to discover the critic's essential position.

There is another reason that, even in spite of its prevalence in his writing, Johnson's figurative language is always in danger of being treated as a form of secondary argument. In early encounters, students immediately notice that Johnson's critical writing seems to move quickly toward bold, encompassing statements: Shakespeare "sacrifices virtue to convenience" (*Johnson on Shakespeare* 7: 71) or "*Paradise Lost* is one of the books which the reader admires and lays down, and forgets to take up again" (*Lives* 1: 183, ed. Hill). Such statements seem almost to do the students' work for them: to have that quality, at once intimidating and inviting, of being willing to declare exactly what they mean in the process of neatly summarizing the texts in which they appear. As a result, students can easily and understandably feel at first that what Johnson's criticism requires of them is agreement or disagreement — but not, in any larger sense, *interpretation*.

To lean against such inclinations and to complicate students' understanding of how Johnson writes literary criticism, I repeatedly focus their attention on Johnson's diction and his selection of images and metaphors, and I insist that they examine the implications of such language with the same imaginative rigor they expect to exercise when interpreting artistic works. In the process, they discover that there are often other strands to Johnson's argument, other ways in which Johnson reports his reactions than in the bold headlines that first attract their attention.

All Johnson's critical texts invite such discussion and reward such an approach. In this course, we examine, for example, the pattern of images Johnson quietly constructs in the Life of Milton to depict him as an aloof and solitary person — images that become central to Johnson's explanation of Milton's epic talents and human deficiencies. We consider some of the more famous and flamboyant images Johnson uses to depict Dryden, Pope, and Cowley. We examine how often Johnson's descriptions of artistic "genius" are associated with travel, with freedom to roam, with metaphors of movement. But for my purposes here, I can perhaps best illustrate the ways of reading I hope to encourage by explaining how we approach his commentary on Shakespeare.

In placement and importance, the Preface to Shakespeare is at the center of the course. After the first of their two readings of it, I ask students what Johnson truly valued as great in Shakespeare. They answer with a sure swiftness that bespeaks their initial confidence in the straightforwardness of Johnson's argument. Always on the lookout (in any course) for the chance to endorse mimetic realism, students emphasize Johnson's praise for Shakespeare's ability to hold up "to his readers a faithful mirrour of manners and of life" (7: 62). Or, with their own sharp inclination toward the innovative, they highlight Johnson's defense of Shakespeare for blending tragedy and comedy and for transcending classical rules of dramatic unity. Or they carefully examine Johnson's tally of Shakespeare's faults and virtues and assure one another that the accounting balances heavily in Shakespeare's favor.

Such claims and responses are, obviously, valid ones: they carefully restate Johnson's explicit critical arguments and identify some essential elements of his appreciation of Shakespeare. They are, therefore, important starting points. But to test their adequacy, I introduce into the discussion Johnson's reactions to particular plays — the tragedies especially. I ask students to consider whether the critical positions they have culled from a reading of the Preface do much to explain the agitation and extremity of Johnson's reaction to *King Lear*, whose events "fill the mind with a perpetual tumult"; to *Othello*, whose death scene "is not to be endured"; to *Hamlet*, whose speeches are for Johnson often "too horrible to be read or to be uttered" (8: 703, 1045, 990).

They start to realize that the cool theoretical arguments that leap out of the Preface on a first reading don't get us very far in explaining the intense turbulence of such reactions. Students begin to think that, like their teacher before another text some years before, they know the Preface's content but haven't discovered its argument.

And so it is at this moment of orchestrated dilemma that I ask students to reread the Preface, paying special attention to the possibility that its figurative language will give us fuller access to Johnson's reaction not only as a critic but as a reader of Shakespeare. I should admit here immediately what I withhold in discussions until much later: that the language and images I select for emphasis are calculated to argue for a particular point of view. I believe that Johnson sees Shakespeare as an aggressive and irresistibly powerful writer, whose virtue and difficulty is his ability to place readers at emotional extremes — to dislocate and transport them into shockingly foreign landscapes. While this vision is embedded in certain aspects of Johnson's pithy claims in the Preface, I believe that it can be fully grasped only by attending carefully to the text's critical metaphors.

After reminding ourselves that Johnson praised Shakespeare for breaking the bonds of genre and ignoring the rules of unity, we resume our discussion by considering Johnson's remark that "such violations of rules merely positive, become the comprehensive genius of Shakespeare" (7: 79). Is there evidence in the Preface to suggest that Johnson means "become" here in both senses? That is, do "such violations" more than flatter the genius of Shakespeare? Do they become the *substance* of that genius?

We can notice that the pattern of diction Johnson uses in the Preface reinforces the vision of Shakespeare as a violator of customs, rules, and traditions. Shakespeare's language and style are called "licentious"; his plots are often "capricious" and "wantonly" produced (7: 56, 515). Johnson employs an image that dramatizes such lawlessness and explains why Shakespeare was free to do as he pleased: "Shakespeare engaged in dramatick poetry *with the world open before him*; the rules of the ancients were yet known to few; the publick judgment was unformed" (7: 69; my emphasis). As memory banks strain to retrieve the Miltonic allusion, we consider why Johnson would analogize Shakespeare and drama to Adam and humankind: both are parents and violators, creators who gain an intelligible identity by breaking the rules.

At the end of the Proposals for Shakespeare and in the Preface itself, Johnson gives us his most explicit title for Shakespeare: "the great father of the English drama" (7: 58, 91). When I ask students to see whether that image is reinforced in the Preface in other ways, they notice that Johnson consistently employs the language of childbirth and parenthood when he talks of Shakespeare's creativity. He writes of the "offspring" of Shakespeare's labors. His plays, Johnson says, were "thrust into the world" (7: 73, 92).

Students start to discover more generally that, throughout the Preface, Johnson recurs to images of paternal power in language and metaphors that stress the deeply masculine character of Shakespeare and his work. They become more alert to the implications of such claims as the one that, to be good readers of Shakespeare's plays, we must shun the private, indoor world traditionally inhabited by women and travel instead in the realms of masculine leisure and business: "He that will understand Shakespeare, must not be content to study him in the closet, he must look for his meaning sometimes among the sports of the field, and sometimes among the manufactures of the shop" (7: 86).

Johnson is especially likely to pursue this line of argument when he is relating Shakespeare to other authors in the tradition. Johnson writes, for example, that Shakespeare "has speeches, perhaps sometimes scenes, which have all the delicacy of Rowe" but "without his effeminacy" (7: 91). After saying that "Addison speaks the language of poets, and Shakespeare, of men," Johnson ranks *Cato* among "the fairest and the noblest progeny which judgment propagates by conjunction with learning." But *Othello* he calls "the vigorous and vivacious offspring of observation impregnated by genius" (7: 84). While Addison, ever delicate and formal, "propagates," Shakespeare — father of English drama — "impregnates."

Johnson's language for Shakespeare is, obviously, more sexually charged; it hints at the aggressive nature of Shakespeare's creative talent and at his explosive assertions of power over his material and, ultimately, over his reader. That this creative power is both exciting and dangerous in Shakespeare's work is implied by Johnson's concluding objection to *Cato*: "Its hopes and fears communicate no vibration to the heart" (7: 84). But Shakespeare, the father, the impregnator, the lawbreaker, can indeed vibrate the heart; he can give life or cause death. He is at once the father and the violator.

Around this point I start to notice a little more shifting in the seats, several raised eyebrows, and a few of those random sidelong glances students have mastered for letting us know when we are in danger of going (or have already gone) too far. But it is important (or so I try to assure them) to notice how the Preface systematically sustains and complicates our vision of Shakespeare's powerful masculinity and paternal authority if we are to grasp how Johnson seeks to explain Shakespeare's radical effect on readers. To examine that effect, I next focus discussion on three moments in the Preface when Johnson, again depending on highly metaphorical language, suggests that this "father of the English drama" is not benign or reassuring but, rather, dangerously alluring and likely to place us at risk.

The first two of these instances I mention only briefly here. Distinguishing Shakespeare from other authors, Johnson writes: "The stream of time, which is continually washing the dissoluble fabricks of other poets, passes without injury by the adamant of Shakespeare" (7: 70). I ask students to consider, in the light of our earlier discussion, why Johnson finds it appropriate to compare Shakespeare to what his *Dictionary* defines as "a stone of impenetrable hardness," to a rock that has the qualities of both a diamond and a lodestone — a rock in a stream whose outer beauty is alluring and whose hidden magnetic power attracts with irresistible force.

The second is this: "The genius of Shakespeare was not to be depressed by the weight of poverty. . . . The incumbrances of his fortune were shaken from his mind, 'as dewdrops from a lion's mane'" (7: 89). We discuss why it might be that, in the course of a text that displays remarkably little interest in Shakespeare's life, Johnson won't allow this ordinary biographical fact to stand alone; he insists on translating it into an image that renews our sense of this poet's powerful dominance. I ask students to consider why Johnson draws his quotation here from a speech, in Shakespeare's *Troilus and Cressida*, condemning a man for being effeminate and urging vigorous, lionlike behavior.

The third is perhaps the most important metaphorical moment in the Preface, not only because it is the most elaborate, but also because it unifies and deepens the implications of the other images Johnson chooses for Shakespeare. Immediately after the comparison of *Cato* with *Othello*, Johnson writes:

> The work of a correct and regular writer is a garden accurately formed and diligently planted, varied with shades, and scented with flowers; the composition of Shakespeare is a forest, in which oaks extend their branches, and pines tower in the air, interspersed sometimes with weeds and brambles, and sometimes giving shelter to myrtles and to roses; filling the eye with awful pomp, and gratifying the mind with endless diversity. Other poets display cabinets of precious rarities, minutely finished, wrought into shape, and polished unto brightness. Shakespeare opens a mine which contains gold and diamonds in unexhaustible plenty, though clouded by incrustations, debased by impurities, and mingled with a mass of meaner minerals.   (7: 84)

Shakespeare's is not a world in which elegant artistic objects might, like mirrors, be "polished unto brightness." It is not the fragile, domestic world of formal cabinets and sculptured gardens; it is, instead, the licentious and primitive world of the forest.

Before the works of lesser poets, Johnson's metaphors assert, our task as readers is essentially calm and contemplative. Like spectators touring a museum, we retain our distance and control as we look at art that has been safely glassed off from the space in which we move. But looking in Shakespeare's world is a far more strenuous and dangerous activity. He makes of us not spectators but travelers: other poets "display" their "cabinets," but Shakespeare "opens a mine," and to see his "gold and diamonds" — to see the "adamant" of Shakespeare — we are required to make a journey within. On that journey we are not allowed to wander along the safely regularized paths of formal gardens. We are forced, instead, to travel in places that we have been taught from childhood are dangerous and threatening: uncharted forests and deep mines, places where we can easily be trapped or lost, buried or abandoned, stalked by lions or lured by gems to fatal depths. We are taken by the father of English drama into a risky mental landscape in which the traveler, like Johnson reading *Macbeth*, "looks round alarmed, and starts to find himself alone" (7: 20).

I conclude the discussion by asking students to look again at the images Johnson uses to open and close the Preface. Our initial encounter with Shakespeare may begin — as the Preface begins — congenially enough, as we look at the mirrored reflection of a familiar and sociable world. But thereafter Johnson's metaphors and diction relentlessly drive us to acknowledge that our encounter with Shakespeare is — like Johnson's own — difficult, strange, inward, and solitary. It is not so much what Shakespeare invites us to see as what he forces us to feel that Johnson seeks to describe. So at the conclusion of the Preface, Johnson adopts a new model for understanding Shakespeare's effect on us and for our role as readers. He prominently features and approvingly quotes Dryden's comment that "when [Shakespeare] describes any thing, you more than see it, you feel it too. . . . He was naturally learned: he needed not the spectacles of books to read nature; he looked inwards, and found her there" (7: 112). The bright polished surfaces are abandoned, and the mine of feeling Shakespeare opens beckons us inward, alone.

Johnson never stopped dreaming "the dreams of a poet"; he never stopped turning to the poet's resources of figurative language when he awoke to find himself a scholar and a critic. He certainly did not confuse criticism with art, but he employed all the devices of art when he sought to articulate his critical judgments. The structure of our courses and the conduct of our discussions should encourage students to remember that Johnson was, first and always, a writer and a reader whose critical reactions were so complicated, rich, and extreme that they required for their expression the varied resources of metaphor. By understanding that, we can better appreciate the talents and strategies that "become the comprehensive genius" of Johnson himself.

CONTRIBUTORS AND SURVEY PARTICIPANTS

Percy G. Adams, *University of Tennessee, Knoxville*
Brenda Ameter, *Troy State University, Dothan*
David R. Anderson, *Florida Atlantic University*
Sheridan Baker, *University of Michigan, Ann Arbor*
James G. Basker, *Barnard College*
Charles L. Batten, *University of California, Los Angeles*
Sophia Blaydes, *West Virginia University, Morgantown*
Edward A. Bloom, *Brown University*
Thomas F. Bonnell, *Saint Mary's College, Indiana*
O M Brack, Jr., *Arizona State University*
John J. Burke, Jr., *University of Alabama, Tuscaloosa*
Cynthia L. Caywood, *University of San Diego*
Michael Cohen, *Murray State University*
Kevin L. Cope, *Louisiana State University, Baton Rouge*
Philip B. Daghlian, *Hilliard, OH*
Bertram H. Davis, *Florida State University*
Frank H. Ellis, *Smith College*
Ann Engar, *University of Utah*
James Engell, *Harvard University*
Timothy Erwin, *University of Nevada, Las Vegas*
Stephen Fix, *Williams College*
Raymond-Jean Frontain, *University of Central Arkansas*
James Gray, *Dalhousie University*
Dustin Griffin, *New York University*
Gloria Sybil Gross, *California State University, Northridge*
Ira Grushow, *Franklin and Marshall College*
Charles H. Hinnant, *University of Missouri, Columbia*
Thomas Jemielity, *University of Notre Dame*
Gwin J. Kolb, *University of Chicago*
Colby H. Kullman, *University of Mississippi*
William Kupersmith, *University of Iowa*
Joanne Lewis, *California State University, Fullerton*
Lawrence Lipking, *Northwestern University*
John L. Mahoney, *Boston College*
Martin Maner, *Wright State University*
Melvyn New, *University of Florida*
Catherine N. Parke, *University of Missouri, Columbia*
R. G. Peterson, *Saint Olaf College*
Allen Reddick, *University of Zurich*
Bruce Redford, *University of Chicago*

Cedric D. Reverand II, *University of Wyoming*
Samuel J. Rogal, *Illinois Valley Community College*
Deborah D. Rogers, *University of Maine, Orono*
Katharine M. Rogers, *American University*
G. S. Rousseau, *University of California, Los Angeles*
William R. Siebenschuh, *Case Western Reserve University*
R. D. Stock, *University of Nebraska, Lincoln*
Albrecht B. Strauss, *University of North Carolina, Chapel Hill*
Linda Troost, *Washington and Jefferson College*
David Wheeler, *University of Southern Mississippi*
Samuel H. Woods, Jr., *Oklahoma State University*

WORKS CITED

Note: Multiple editions are listed in chronological order.

Abrams, M. H. *The Mirror and the Lamp: Romantic Theory and the Critical Tradition*. 1953. New York: Oxford UP, 1958.

Abrams, M. H., et al., eds. *The Norton Anthology of English Literature*. 4th ed. Vol. 1. New York: Norton, 1979.

———, eds. *The Norton Anthology of English Literature*. 5th ed. Vol. 1. New York: Norton, 1986.

———, eds. *The Norton Anthology of English Literature*. 6th ed. Vol. 1. New York: Norton, 1993.

———, eds. *The Norton Anthology of English Literature: Major Authors Edition*. 5th ed. New York: Norton, 1987.

Alkon, Paul Kent. *Samuel Johnson and Moral Discipline*. Evanston: Northwestern UP, 1967.

Bailey, Nathan. *An Universal Etymological English Dictionary*. London, 1721.

Balderston, Katherine C. "Johnson's Vile Melancholy." *The Age of Johnson: Essays Presented to Chauncey B. Tinker*. Ed. F. W. Hilles. New Haven: Yale UP, 1949. 3–14.

Barber, C. L. *Creating Elizabethan Tragedy*. Chicago: U of Chicago P, 1988.

Barber, C. L., and Richard P. Wheeler. *The Whole Journey: Shakespeare's Power of Development*. Berkeley: U of California P, 1986.

Bate, Walter Jackson. *The Achievement of Samuel Johnson*. Oxford: Oxford UP, 1955.

———. *From Classic to Romantic*. 1946. New York: Harper, 1961.

———. *Samuel Johnson*. New York: Harcourt, 1977.

———, ed. *Selected Essays from the* Rambler, Adventurer, *and* Idler. New Haven: Yale UP, 1968.

Beckson, Karl, and Arthur Ganz. *Literary Terms: A Dictionary*. 3rd ed. New York: Noonday-Farrar, 1989.

Bloom, Edward A. *Samuel Johnson in Grub Street*. Providence: Brown UP, 1957.

Bloom, Edward A., and Lillian D. Bloom. "Johnson's 'Mournful Narrative': The Rhetoric of 'London.'" Bond 107–44.

Bloom, Harold. *The Visionary Company*. Rev. ed. Ithaca: Cornell UP, 1971.

Bogel, Frederick. "Johnson and the Role of Authority." *The New Eighteenth Century: Theory, Politics, English Literature*. Ed. Felicity Nussbaum and Laura Brown. New York: Methuen, 1987. 189–209.

Boileau-Despréaux, Nicolas. *Œuvres complètes*. Paris: Gallimard, 1966.

Bond, W. H., ed. *Eighteenth-Century Studies in Honor of Donald F. Hyde*. New York: Grolier, 1970.

Boswell, James. *The Life of Johnson*. Ed. George Birkbeck Hill and L. F. Powell. 2nd ed. 6 vols. Oxford: Clarendon–Oxford UP, 1934–64.

———. *The Life of Johnson*. Ed. R. W. Chapman. Rev. J. D. Fleeman. Oxford: Oxford UP, 1980.

———. *London Journal, 1762–1763*. Ed. Frederick A. Pottle. New York: McGraw, 1950.

Boswell's London Journal. 2 parts. Yale Films, 1985.

Boyce, Benjamin. "Johnson's *Life of Savage* and Its Literary Background." *Studies in Philology* 53 (1956): 576–98.

Brack, Gae Annette. "Samuel Johnson and Four Literary Women." Diss. Arizona State U, 1979.

Brack, O M, Jr., and Robert E. Kelley, eds. *Early Biographies of Samuel Johnson*. Iowa City: U of Iowa P, 1974.

Brady, Frank, and W. K. Wimsatt, eds. *Samuel Johnson: Selected Poetry and Prose*. Berkeley: U of California P, 1977.

Bronson, Bertrand. "The Double Tradition of Dr. Johnson." *ELH* 18 (1951): 90–106.

———. "Johnson Agonistes." *Johnson Agonistes and Other Essays*. 1944. Berkeley: U of California P, 1965. 1–52.

———, ed. *Samuel Johnson: Rasselas, Poems, and Selected Prose*. 3rd ed. San Francisco: Holt, Rinehart, 1971.

Brown, Joseph Epes. *Critical Opinions of Samuel Johnson*. 1926. Princeton: Princeton UP, 1967.

Brownell, Morris R. *Samuel Johnson's Attitude to the Arts*. Oxford: Clarendon–Oxford UP, 1989.

Brownley, Martine Watson. " 'Under the Dominion of Some Woman': The Friendship of Samuel Johnson and Hester Thrale." *Mothering the Mind: Twelve Studies of Writers and Their Silent Partners*. Ed. Ruth Perry and Martine Watson Brownley. New York: Holmes, 1984. 64–79.

Burke, John J., Jr., and Donald Kay, eds. *The Unknown Samuel Johnson*. Madison: U of Wisconsin P, 1983.

Burney, Charles. *Account of the Commemoration of Handel*. London, 1785.

Butt, John. *Biography in the Hands of Walton, Johnson, and Boswell*. Ewing Lectures, 1962. Los Angeles: U of California P, 1966.

Butt, John, and Geoffrey Carnall. *The Mid-Eighteenth Century*. Vol. 8 of *The Oxford History of English Literature*. Oxford: Clarendon–Oxford UP, 1979.

Chapin, Chester F. *The Religious Thought of Samuel Johnson*. Ann Arbor: U of Michigan P, 1968.

Chapman, R. W., ed. "The Formal Parts of Johnson's Letters." *Essays on the Eighteenth Century Presented to David Nichol Smith in Honour of His Seventieth Birthday*. Oxford: Clarendon–Oxford UP, 1945. 147–54.

Chapman, R. W., and Allen T. Hazen. "Johnsonian Bibliography: A Supplement to Courtney." *Proceedings of the Oxford Bibliographical Society* 5 (1939): 119–66.

Clark, Kenneth. *Civilisation: A Personal View*. New York: Harper, 1969.

————. *The Worship of Nature. Civilisation.* BBC Films, 1970.

Clifford, James L. *Dictionary Johnson: Samuel Johnson's Middle Years.* New York: McGraw, 1979.

————. *Young Sam Johnson.* New York: McGraw, 1955.

Clifford, James L., and Donald J. Greene. *Samuel Johnson: A Survey and Bibliography of Critical Studies.* Minneapolis: U of Minnesota P, 1970.

Conrad, Joseph. *Lord Jim.* Boston: Houghton, 1958.

Coupland, Reginald. *The British Anti-slavery Movement.* 2nd ed. London: Cass, 1964.

Courtney, William P., and David Nichol Smith. *Bibliography of Samuel Johnson.* 1915. Reissued (with illus.). Oxford: Clarendon–Oxford UP, 1925.

Critical Review 3 (1757): 439–48.

Curley, Thomas M. *Samuel Johnson and the Age of Travel.* Athens: U of Georgia P, 1976.

Damrosch, Leopold. *Samuel Johnson and the Tragic Sense.* Princeton: Princeton UP, 1972.

————. *The Uses of Johnson's Criticism.* Charlottesville: U of Virginia P, 1976.

Defoe, Daniel. *A Tour through the Whole Island of Great Britain.* Ed. Pat Rogers. Baltimore: Penguin, 1971.

DeMaria, Robert, Jr. *Johnson's* Dictionary *and the Language of Learning.* Chapel Hill: U of North Carolina P, 1986.

————. "The Theory of Language in Johnson's *Dictionary.*" Korshin 159–74.

Eddy, Donald. *Samuel Johnson: Book Reviewer in the "Literary Magazine; or, Universal Review," 1756–1758.* New York: Garland, 1979.

Edinger, William. *Samuel Johnson and Poetic Style.* Chicago: U of Chicago P, 1977.

Eliot, T. S. Introduction. London: A Poem *and* The Vanity of Human Wishes. By Samuel Johnson. London: Etchells, 1930. Rpt. as "Poetry in the Eighteenth Century." *The Pelican Guide to English Literature.* Vol. 4. Harmondsworth, Eng.: Penguin, 1957. 271–77.

————. "Johnson as Critic and Poet." *On Poetry and Poets.* London: Faber, 1957. 162–92.

Erwin, Timothy. "Johnson's *Life of Savage* and Lockean Psychology." *Studies in Eighteenth-Century Culture* 18 (1988): 199–212.

Evans, Bergen B. "Dr. Johnson's Theory of Biography." *Review of English Studies* 10 (1934): 301–10.

Fielding, Henry. *The History of Tom Jones, a Foundling.* Ed. Martin C. Battestin. Middletown: Wesleyan UP, 1975.

————. *Joseph Andrews.* Ed. Martin C. Battestin. Middletown: Wesleyan UP, 1967.

Fleeman, J. D., ed. *A Preliminary Handlist of Documents and Manuscripts of Samuel Johnson.* Occasional Publications 2. Oxford: Oxford Bibliographical Soc., 1967.

Folkenflik, Robert. *Samuel Johnson, Biographer.* Ithaca: Cornell UP, 1978.

Fussell, Paul. *Samuel Johnson and the Life of Writing.* New York: Harcourt, 1971.

George, M. Dorothy. *London Life in the Eighteenth Century.* 1925. Chicago: Academy Chicago, 1984.

Gide, André. *The Counterfeiters.* New York: Random, 1955.

Golden, Morris. *The Self Observed: Swift, Johnson, Wordsworth.* Baltimore: Johns Hopkins UP, 1972.

Gray, James. *Johnson's Sermons: A Study.* Oxford: Clarendon–Oxford UP, 1972.

Greene, Donald J. *The Age of Exuberance: Backgrounds to Eighteenth-Century English Literature.* New York: Random, 1970.

———. "Johnson's Contributions to the *Literary Magazine.*" *Review of English Studies* 7 (1956): 376.

———. *The Politics of Samuel Johnson.* 1960. 2nd ed. New Haven: Yale UP, 1990.

———, ed. *Samuel Johnson.* Oxford Authors. Oxford: Oxford UP, 1984.

———. *Samuel Johnson.* Twayne's English Authors Series. 1970. Rev. ed. New York: Twayne, 1989.

———, ed. *Samuel Johnson: A Collection of Critical Essays.* Twentieth-Century Views. Englewood Cliffs: Prentice, 1965.

Greene, Donald J., and John A. Vance. *A Bibliography of Johnsonian Studies, 1970–1985.* ELS Monograph Series 39. Victoria, B.C.: U of Victoria, 1987.

Gregory, John. *A Father's Legacy to His Daughter.* London, 1774.

Gross, Gloria Sybil. *This Invisible Riot of the Mind: Samuel Johnson's Psychological Theory.* Philadelphia: U of Pennsylvania P, 1992.

Grundy, Isobel. *Samuel Johnson and the Scale of Greatness.* Athens: U of Georgia P, 1986.

———. "Samuel Johnson as Patron of Women." *The Age of Johnson* 1 (1987): 59–77.

———. "The Techniques of Spontaneity: Johnson's Developing Epistolary Style." Korshin 211–24.

Hagstrum, Jean H. *Samuel Johnson's Literary Criticism.* 1952. Chicago: U of Chicago P, 1967.

Hansen, Marlene. "Sex and Love, Marriage and Friendship: A Feminist Reading of the Quest for Happiness in *Rasselas.*" *English Studies* 66 (1985): 513–26.

Hawkins, John. *The Life of Samuel Johnson, LL.D.* London, 1787.

Hazen, Allen T., ed. *Samuel Johnson's Prefaces and Dedications.* New Haven: Yale UP, 1937.

Hedrick, Elizabeth. "Locke's Theory of Language and Johnson's *Dictionary.*" *Eighteenth-Century Studies* 20 (1987): 422–44.

Hill, G. B., ed. *Johnsonian Miscellanies.* 2 vols. 1897. New York: Barnes, 1966.

Hilles, Frederick W., ed. *The Age of Johnson: Essays Presented to Chauncey Brewster Tinker.* New Haven: Yale UP, 1949.

———, ed. *New Light on Dr. Johnson: Essays on the Occasion of His 250th Birthday.* New Haven: Yale UP, 1959.

Hoover, Benjamin B. *Samuel Johnson's Parliamentary Reporting*. U of California Pub. 7. Berkeley: U of California P, 1953.

Hudson, Nicholas. *Samuel Johnson and Eighteenth-Century Thought*. Oxford: Clarendon–Oxford UP, 1988.

Hyde, Mary. *The Impossible Friendship: Boswell and Mrs. Thrale*. Cambridge: Harvard UP, 1972.

———. *The Thrales of Streatham Park*. Cambridge: Harvard UP, 1977.

Irwin, George. *Samuel Johnson: A Personality in Conflict*. Auckland: Auckland UP, 1971.

Jemielity, Thomas. "Samuel Johnson, *The Vanity of Human Wishes*, and Biographical Criticism." *Studies in Eighteenth-Century Culture* 15 (1986): 227–39.

Jenyns, Soame. *A Free Inquiry into the Nature and Origin of Evil*. 1757. Facsimile rpt. in *British Philosophers and Theologians of the Seventeenth and Eighteenth Centuries*. Ed. René Wellek. New York: Garland, 1976.

Johnson, Claudia L. "Samuel Johnson's Moral Psychology and Locke's 'Of Power.'" *SEL* 24 (1984): 563–82.

Johnson, Samuel. "Debates in the Senate of Magna Lilliputia." *Gentleman's Magazine* 8 (June 1738): 285–86.

———. *Diaries, Prayers, and Annals*. Ed. E. L. McAdam, Jr., Donald Hyde, and Mary Hyde. Vol. 1 of Yale Edition of the Works of Samuel Johnson. New Haven: Yale UP, 1958.

———. *Dictionary of the English Language*. London, 1755. 2 vols., folio.

———. *Dictionary of the English Language . . . Abstracted from the Folio Edition*. London, 1756. 2 vols., octavo.

———. *Dictionary of the English Language*. Photographic reprod. of mixed set of 1st and 2nd ed. sheets. 2 vols. New York: AMS, 1967.

———. *Dictionary of the English Language*. Photographic reprod. of 1755 ed. Hildesheim, W. Ger.: Olms, 1968.

———. *Dictionary of the English Language*. Introd. James L. Clifford. Photographic reprod. of 4th ed., 1773. Beirut: Librairie du Liban, 1978.

———. *Dictionary of the English Language*. Photographic reprod. of mixed set of 1st and 2nd ed. sheets. 1967. London: Times, 1979.

———. *Dictionary of the English Language*. Photographic reprod. of 1755 ed. Tokyo: Yoshudo, 1983.

———. *Dictionary of the English Language*. Photographic reprod. of 1755 ed. 2 vols. Harlow, Eng.: Longman, 1990.

———. *The History of Rasselas, Prince of Abissinia*. Harmondsworth, Eng.: Penguin, 1976.

———. *The History of Rasselas, Prince of Abissinia*. Oxford: Oxford UP, 1988.

———. *The Idler and the Adventurer*. Ed. W. J. Bate, John M. Bullitt, and L. F. Powell. Vol. 2 of Yale Edition of the Works of Samuel Johnson. New Haven: Yale UP, 1963.

———. *Johnson on Shakespeare*. Ed. Arthur Sherbo. Introd. Bertrand H. Bronson. Vols. 7–8 of Yale Edition of the Works of Samuel Johnson. New Haven: Yale UP, 1968.

———. *A Journey to the Western Islands of Scotland*. Ed. Mary Lascelles. Vol. 9 of Yale Edition of the Works of Samuel Johnson. New Haven: Yale UP, 1971.

———. *A Journey to the Western Islands of Scotland*. Introd. and notes by J. D. Fleeman. Oxford: Clarendon–Oxford UP, 1985.

———. *The Letters of Samuel Johnson with Mrs. Thrale's Genuine Letters to Him*. Ed. R. W. Chapman. 3 vols. London: Oxford UP, 1952.

———. *The Letters of Samuel Johnson*. Hyde Edition. Ed. Bruce Redford. 5 vols. Princeton: Princeton UP, 1991–93.

———. *Life of Savage*. Ed. Clarence Tracy. Oxford: Clarendon–Oxford UP, 1971.

———. *Lives of the English Poets*. Ed. George Birkbeck Hill. 3 vols. Oxford: Clarendon–Oxford UP, 1905.

———. *Lives of the English Poets*. Ed. Ernest Rhys. 2 vols. New York: Dutton, 1925.

———. *Poems*. Ed. E. L. McAdam, Jr., and George Milne. Vol. 6 of Yale Edition of the Works of Samuel Johnson. New Haven: Yale UP, 1964.

———. *Poems of Samuel Johnson*. Ed. David Nichol Smith and Edward L. McAdam, Jr. 1941. 2nd ed. Oxford: Clarendon–Oxford UP, 1974.

———. *Political Writings*. Ed. Donald J. Greene. Vol. 10 of Yale Edition of the Works of Samuel Johnson. New Haven: Yale UP, 1977.

———. *Prefaces, Biographical and Critical, to the Works of the English Poets*. 10 vols. London, 1779–81.

———. *The Rambler*. Ed. W. J. Bate and Albrecht B. Strauss. Vols. 3–5 of Yale Edition of the Works of Samuel Johnson. New Haven: Yale UP, 1969.

———. *Rasselas*. Ed. J. P. Hardy. London: Oxford UP, 1968.

———. *Rasselas and Other Tales* ("The Vision of Theodore" and "The Fountains"). Ed. Gwin J. Kolb. Vol. 16 of Yale Edition of the Works of Samuel Johnson. New Haven: Yale UP, 1990.

———. Rev. of *A Free Inquiry into the Nature and Origin of Evil*, by Soame Jenyns. *The Literary Magazine; or, Universal Review* 13–15 (Apr.–July 1757): 171–75, 251–53, 301–06.

———. *Samuel Johnson: The Complete English Poems*. Ed. J. D. Fleeman. 1971. New Haven: Yale UP, 1982.

———. *Sermons*. Ed. Jean H. Hagstrum and James Gray. Vol. 14 of Yale Edition of the Works of Samuel Johnson. New Haven: Yale UP, 1978.

———. *A Voyage to Abyssinia*. Ed. Joel Gold. Vol. 15 of Yale Edition of the Works of Samuel Johnson. New Haven: Yale UP, 1985.

———. *The Works of Samuel Johnson, LL.D.* 9 vols. London: Pickering, 1825.

Johnson, Samuel, and James Boswell. *A Journey to the Western Islands of Scotland* and *Journal of a Tour to the Hebrides with Samuel Johnson, LL.D.* Ed. Allan Wendt. Boston: Houghton, 1965.

———. *A Journey to the Western Islands of Scotland* and *The Journal of a Tour to the Hebrides*. Ed. and introd. Peter Levi. New York: Penguin, 1984.

Kaminski, Thomas. *The Early Career of Samuel Johnson*. Oxford: Oxford UP, 1987.

Keast, W. R. "The Theoretical Foundations of Johnson's Criticism." *Critics and Criticism, Ancient and Modern*. Ed. R. S. Crane. 1952. Chicago: U of Chicago P, 1975. 389–407.

Kelly, Joan. *Women, History and Theory: The Essays of Joan Kelly*. Chicago: U of Chicago P, 1984.

Kernan, Alvin. *Printing Technology, Letters, and Samuel Johnson*. Princeton: Princeton UP, 1987.

Kolb, Gwin. "*The Vision of Theodore*: Genre, Context, Early Reception." *Johnson and His Age*. Ed. James Engell. Cambridge: Harvard UP, 1984. 107–24.

Korshin, Paul J., ed. *Johnson after Two Hundred Years*. Philadelphia: U of Pennsylvania P, 1986.

Krieger, Murray. *The Classic Vision: The Retreat from Extremity in Modern Literature*. Baltimore: Johns Hopkins UP, 1971.

Krutch, Joseph Wood. *Samuel Johnson*. New York: Henry Holt, 1944.

Kupersmith, William. "Declamatory Grandeur: Johnson and Juvenal." *Arion* 9 (1970): 66–72.

Lane, Margaret. "The President's Address." *Transactions of the Johnson Society of Lichfield* (Dec. 1971): 30–45.

Lascelles, Mary. "Johnson's Last Allusion to Mary, Queen of Scots." *Review of English Studies* 8 (1957): 32–37.

———. "Some Reflections on Johnson's Hebridean Journey." *New Rambler: Journal of the Johnson Society of London* (June 1961): 2–13.

Lascelles, Mary, James L. Clifford, J. D. Fleeman, and John P. Hardy, eds. *Johnson, Boswell, and Their Circle: Essays Presented to Lawrence Fitzroy Powell in Honour of His Eighty-Fourth Birthday*. Oxford: Oxford UP, 1965.

Leavis, F. R. "Johnson as Critic." Greene, *Collection* 70–88.

———. "Johnson as Poet." *The Common Pursuit*. New York: Stewart, 1952. 116–20.

Lewis, C. S. *Rehabilitations and Other Essays*. London: Oxford UP, 1939.

Lipking, Lawrence. "Learning to Read Johnson: *The Vision of Theodore* and *The Vanity of Human Wishes*." *ELH* 43 (1976): 517–37. Rpt. in *Modern Essays on Eighteenth-Century Literature*. Ed. Leopold Damrosch, Jr. New York: Oxford UP, 1988. 335–54.

Livingston, Chella Courington. "Samuel Johnson's Literary Treatment of Women." Diss. U of South Carolina, 1985.

Locke, John. *Essay concerning Human Understanding*. Ed. Peter H. Nidditch. Oxford: Clarendon–Oxford UP, 1975.

Lonsdale, Roger, ed. *The New Oxford Book of Eighteenth-Century Verse*. Oxford: Oxford UP, 1984.

Lorch, Jennifer. *Mary Wollstonecraft: The Making of a Radical Feminist*. New York: Berg, 1990.

Lovejoy, Arthur O. *The Great Chain of Being: A Study of the History of an Idea*. Cambridge: Harvard UP, 1936.

Macaulay, Thomas Babington. "Life of Johnson." *Encyclopaedia Britannica*. 1856 ed.

——. Rev. of Boswell's *Life of Johnson*, ed. John Wilson Croker. Edinburgh Review (Sept. 1831).

Mack, Maynard. *Alexander Pope: A Life*. New York: Norton, 1985.

MacLean, Kenneth. *John Locke and English Literature of the Eighteenth Century*. New Haven: Yale UP, 1936.

Mandelbaum, Allen. Introduction. *Dante:* Inferno. Berkeley: U of California P, 1980. x–xxiv.

Marcus, Jane. *Art and Anger: Reading like a Woman*. Columbus: Ohio State UP, 1988.

Martin, Martin. *A Description of the Western Islands of Scotland*. 2nd ed. London: Bell, 1716.

McCamic, Charles. *Doctor Samuel Johnson and the American Colonies*. Rowfantia 10. Cleveland: Rowfant Club, 1925.

McDavid, Raven I., Jr. "Usage, Dialects, and Functional Varieties." *The Random House College Dictionary*. Rev. ed. New York: Random, 1988. xix–xxi.

McFarland, Thomas. *Romanticism and the Forms of Ruin: Wordsworth, Coleridge, and Modalities of Fragmentation*. Princeton: Princeton UP, 1980.

McIntosh, Carey. *The Choice of Life: Samuel Johnson and the World of Fiction*. New Haven: Yale UP, 1973.

McLaverty, James. "From Definition to Explanation: Locke's Influence on Johnson's *Dictionary*." *Journal of the History of Ideas* 47 (1986): 377–94.

Meyer, Bernard C. "Notes on Flying and Dying." *Psychoanalytic Quarterly* 52 (1983): 327–52.

Miller, J. Hillis. *The Disappearance of God*. Cambridge: Harvard UP, 1963.

Nath, Prem, ed. *Fresh Reflections on Samuel Johnson*. Troy: Whitston, 1987.

New, Melvyn, ed. *Approaches to Teaching Sterne's* Tristram Shandy. New York: MLA, 1989.

Newton, Peter M. "Samuel Johnson's Breakdown and Recovery in Middle-Age: A Life Span Developmental Approach to Mental Illness and Its Cure." *International Review of Psychoanalysis* 11 (1984): 93–118.

Novak, Maximillian E. *Eighteenth-Century English Literature*. New York: Schocken, 1984.

O'Donnell, Sheryl Rae. " 'Born to Know, to Reason, and to Act': Samuel Johnson's Attitude toward Women as Reflected in His Writings." Diss. U of Arizona, 1979.

——. " 'Tricked Out for Sale': Samuel Johnson's Attitude toward Prostitution." *Transactions of the Samuel Johnson Society of the Northwest* 9 (1978): 119–35.

Piozzi, Hester Lynch Thrale. *Anecdotes of Samuel Johnson*. Ed. S. C. Roberts. Cambridge: Cambridge UP, 1932.

Piper, William Bowman. *The Heroic Couplet*. Cleveland: P of Case Western Reserve U, 1969.

Pope, Alexander. *The Correspondence of Alexander Pope*. Ed. George Sherburn. 5 vols. Oxford: Clarendon–Oxford UP, 1956.

——. *An Essay on Man*. Ed. Maynard Mack. London: Methuen, 1950.

Porter, Roy. *English Society of the Eighteenth Century*. London: Lane, 1982.

———. " 'The Hunger of Imagination': Approaching Samuel Johnson's Melancholy." *The Anatomy of Madness: Essays in the History of Psychiatry.* Ed. W. F. Bynum, Roy Porter, and Michael Shepherd. Vol. 1. London: Tavistock, 1985. 63–102. 2 vols.

Price, Martin. *To the Palace of Wisdom: Studies in Order and Energy from Dryden to Blake.* New York: Doubleday, 1964.

Quinlan, Maurice J. *Samuel Johnson: A Layman's Religion.* Madison: U of Wisconsin P, 1964.

Raleigh, Walter. *Six Essays on Johnson.* Oxford: Clarendon–Oxford UP, 1910.

Reade, Aleyn Lyell. *Johnsonian Gleanings.* 1909–52. New York: Octagon, 1967.

Reddick, Allen. *The Making of Johnson's Dictionary, 1746–1773.* Cambridge: Cambridge UP, 1990.

Redford, Bruce. *The Converse of the Pen: Acts of Intimacy in the Eighteenth-Century Familiar Letter.* Chicago: U of Chicago P, 1986.

———. "Samuel Johnson and Mrs. Thrale: The 'Little Language' of the Public Moralist." *Converse* 206–43.

Rich, Adrienne. "Snapshots of a Daughter-in-Law." *The Fact of a Doorframe: Poems Selected and New 1950–84.* New York: Norton, 1984. 35–39.

Richardson, Jonathan. *The Life of Milton.* 1734. *The Early Lives of Milton.* Ed. Helen Darbishire. New York: Barnes, 1965. 199–330.

Ricks, Christopher. "Allusion: The Poet as Heir." *Studies in the Eighteenth Century* 3. Ed. R. F. Brissenden and J. C. Eade. Canberra: Australian National UP, 1976. 209–40.

Riely, John C. "Johnson and Mrs. Thrale: The Beginning and the End." *Johnson and His Age.* Ed. James Engell. Harvard English Studies 12. Cambridge: Harvard UP, 1984.

Rogers, Katharine. *Feminism in Eighteenth-Century England.* Urbana: U of Illinois P, 1982.

Rompkey, Ronald. *Soame Jenyns.* Boston: Twayne, 1984.

Sachs, Arieh. *Passionate Intelligence: Imagination and Reason in the Work of Samuel Johnson.* Baltimore: Johns Hopkins UP, 1967.

Sacks, Sheldon. *Fiction and the Shape of Belief: A Study of Henry Fielding with Glances at Swift, Johnson, and Richardson.* Berkeley: U of California P, 1964.

Sambrook, James. *The Eighteenth Century: The Intellectual and Cultural Context of English Literature, 1700–1789.* London: Longman, 1986.

Schwartz, Richard B. *Daily Life in Johnson's London.* Madison: U of Wisconsin P, 1983.

———. *Samuel Johnson and the Problem of Evil.* Madison: U of Wisconsin P, 1975.

Sherburn, George, and Donald F. Bond. *The Restoration and Eighteenth Century.* Vol. 3 of *A Literary History of England.* Ed. Albert C. Baugh. 2nd ed. New York: Appleton, 1967.

Sledd, James H., and Gwin J. Kolb. *Dr. Johnson's Dictionary: Essays in the Biography of a Book.* Chicago: U of Chicago P, 1955.

Smith, David Nichol. "Johnson and Boswell." *The Age of Johnson.* 1913. Vol. 10 in *The Cambridge History of English Literature.* Ed. A. W. Ward and A. R. Waller. Cambridge: Cambridge UP, 1907–17.

———. "Samuel Johnson's Poems." *Review of English Studies* 19 (1943): 44–50.

Sprat, Thomas. *An Account of the Life and Writings of Mr. Abraham Cowley.* 1668. *Critical Essays of the Seventeenth Century.* Ed. J. E. Spingarn. Vol. 2. Bloomington: Indiana UP, 1957. 119–46.

Stephen, Leslie. *History of English Thought in the Eighteenth Century.* Vol. 1. London: Smith, 1876. 2 vols.

Tillotson, Geoffrey, Paul Fussell, Jr., and Marshall Waingrow, eds. *Eighteenth-Century English Literature.* San Diego: Harcourt, 1969.

Turberville, A. S., ed. *Johnson's England: An Account of the Life and Manners of His Age.* 2 vols. Oxford: Clarendon–Oxford UP, 1933.

Vance, John A. *Samuel Johnson and the Sense of History.* Athens: U of Georgia P, 1984.

Vergil. *Aeneid. Vergili Opera.* Ed. R. A. B. Mynors. Oxford: Clarendon–Oxford UP, 1969.

Voitle, Robert. *Samuel Johnson the Moralist.* Cambridge: Harvard UP, 1961.

Voltaire. Candide *and Other Writings.* Ed. Haskell M. Block. New York: Modern Library, 1956.

Wain, John. "Dr. Johnson's Poetry." *A House for the Truth: Critical Essays.* New York: Viking, 1973. 105–27.

———. *Samuel Johnson.* New York: Viking, 1975.

Walesby, Francis Pearson, ed. *The Works of Samuel Johnson, LL.D.* 11 vols. Oxford: Talboys, 1825.

Walker, Ralph C. S. *The Coherence Theory of Truth: Realism, Anti-realism, Idealism.* London: Routledge, 1989.

Walker, Robert G. *Eighteenth-Century Arguments for Immortality and Johnson's Rasselas.* ELS Monograph Series 9. Victoria, B.C.: U of Victoria, 1977.

Watkins, W. B. C. *Johnson and English Poetry before 1660.* 1936. Princeton: Princeton UP, 1965.

———. *Perilous Balance: The Tragic Genius of Swift, Johnson, and Sterne.* Princeton: Princeton UP, 1939.

Watson, George, and I. R. Willison, eds. *New Cambridge Bibliography of English Literature.* 5 vols. Cambridge: Cambridge UP, 1969–77.

Weinbrot, Howard D. *The Formal Strain: Studies in Augustan Imitation and Satire.* Chicago: U of Chicago P, 1969.

Wellington, Charmaine. "Dr. Johnson's Attitude towards the Education of Women." *New Rambler* serial C 18 (1977): 49–58.

Willey, Basil. *The Eighteenth-Century Background: Studies on the Idea of Nature in the Thought of the Period.* London: Chatto, 1940.

Williams, Raymond. *Keywords: A Vocabulary of Culture and Society.* 2nd ed. London: Fontana, 1983.

Wilson, Mona, ed. *Johnson: Prose and Poetry.* Cambridge: Harvard UP, 1967.

Wiltshire, John. *Samuel Johnson in the Medical World: The Doctor and the Patient.* Cambridge: Cambridge UP, 1991.

Wimsatt, W. K., Jr. *Philosophic Words: A Study of Style and Meaning in the* Rambler *and* Dictionary *of Samuel Johnson.* New Haven: Yale UP, 1948.

———. *The Prose Style of Samuel Johnson.* Yale Studies in English 94. New Haven: Yale UP, 1941.

Wood, Neal. *The Politics of Locke's Philosophy.* Berkeley: U of California P, 1983.

Yolton, John. *Locke: An Introduction.* London: Blackwell, 1985.

INDEX